W9-CCQ-161

The Commander's Palace

New Orleans Cookbook

ELLA & DICK BRENNAN

The Commander's Palace *New Orleans Cookbook*

Text with Lynne Roberts • Illustrations by Arthur Shilstone

Clarkson N. Potter, Inc./Publishers
DISTRIBUTED BY CROWN PUBLISHERS, INC., NEW YORK

Published by Clarkson N. Potter, Inc., 225 Park Avenue South, New York, New York 10003 and represented in Canada by the Canadian MANDA Group.

Manufactured in the United States of America

Library of Congress Cataloging-in-Publication Data

Brennan, Ella.
The Commander's Palace New Orleans cookbook.

Includes index.
1. Cookery, American—Louisiana. 2. Commander's Palace (Restaurant) I. Brennan, Dick. II. Roberts, Lynne. III. Title.
TX715.B8384 1984 641.59763 83-16022
ISBN 0-517-55049-0

Designed by Stephanie Tevonian, Works.

10 9 8

To Adelaide, our sister, whose generosity, love, and understanding encouraged us all.

With love,
Ella, Dick, John, and Dottie

And grateful acknowledgment to our extended family, who have supported and encouraged us in our efforts to make Commander's Palace a restaurant where we all can work to reach our goals of excellence. We would especially like to mention Jill Rouse, David Guglielmo, George Rico, Floyd Bealer, and James Tanner.

Contents

Introduction viii

Drinks 1

Appetizers and Soups 12

Salads 49

Egg Dishes 68

Seafood 84

Chicken and Game 121

Beef and Veal 140

Desserts and Coffees 161

Lagniappe: Seasonings, Stocks, and Sauces 188

Index 200

Introduction

A Family Tradition

In the Brennan family, food and fabulous feasts have always been a part of life. Mother was a marvelous cook, and with six children around the dinner table, meals were always a happy time. Perhaps part of our combined passion for the restaurant business has come from a desire to recreate and recapture the comforting feelings of coziness and warmth we all felt during childhood.

Sunday night we would always have a big supper. One of Mother's specialties, and a family favorite even today, is boeuf en daube, a classic French beef stew—only she made it with veal and Creole seasonings. With that came fresh vegetables, salad, hot, newly baked bread, and lots of desserts. There was ordinary food at other people's houses; then there was Mother's cooking.

It was very important to her to use only the best and freshest local ingredients. Mr. Tony, the vegetable man, would drive up to the house with his horse and wagon practically every day. He would go around the side of the house and into the kitchen, where he would sit at the table with Mother and have coffee. Then she would go out to his cart, filled with brightly colored fruits and vegetables, and buy whatever was best that day—lush red Creole tomatoes, juicy sweet watermelons, bright green okra, and deep purple eggplant. Today, we plan the weekly menus and daily specials at Commander's in much the same way. We used to watch Mother carefully sorting through the vegetables and examining the fruit. She was uncompromising in demanding quality, and believed that if you couldn't have food fresh, you shouldn't serve it at all—something we believe strongly at the restaurant.

Another great cook we learned from was Leona Nichols, who worked for Mother in those days. There was always lots of preparation going on, and we all liked to sit at the kitchen table and observe her stuffing eggplants with seafood, shrimp, or crawfish, making deviled crab cakes, or cooking marvelous shrimp or the tiniest soft-shell crabs fresh from the market. On Saturdays she would sometimes bake a ham and serve it with homemade potato salad, or make panéed veal cutlets, and we would all sit around the big dinner table and feast.

When we got a little older we were thrilled to be sent for fresh ingredients down the street at an absolutely marvelous grocery store. In those days, of course, everything was fresh. Prior to Christmas, Leona would do lots of baking—Christmas cakes, cookies, and candies—and would send us to the store with a list of things like dried fruits, dates, and

---

A table in the glass-walled Garden Room of the restaurant looks out through the branches of a two-hundred-year-old oak tree.

other exotica (to us) like ginger. We loved to wander around the store, exploring, looking, smelling, touching, and tasting all the strange and wonderful new ingredients. This too was part of our education. The reward for our labors would come later, when we were at home studying, and a sweet-scented aroma wafting from the oven would announce a wonderful fresh Christmas cake or cookies to nibble on. There were always great quantities of home-baked cakes and cookies, muffins and rolls, pies and puddings.

Holidays like Christmas, Thanksgiving, New Year's, and Mardi Gras inspired special menus and favorite dishes, and the festivity of the food created a relaxed atmosphere of culinary celebration. Today, at Commander's, we have tried to continue that family tradition with special holiday menus, our Jazz Brunch (complete with live music and colored balloons), and our celebration dessert, the richest (and most popular) on the menu.

Besides holidays, special dishes at home might be occasioned by a local fisherman bringing in a particularly fine catch of soft-shell crabs, brother Dick and his friends going crawfishing after a heavy rain, or Father bringing home a beautiful brace of fresh wild ducks. Louisiana is a very big fishing and hunting area. Even today, people come from all over to go duck hunting.

Later, when we were in high school during World War II, Leona would send us down to the butcher shop to pick out the meat. Behind the meat counter was a beautiful sign in colored tiles that said, "Good Will is the disposition of a pleased customer to return where he's been well served." We stood there waiting so often that the saying became engraved in our minds. To this day, our standard rule is, if a customer complains, pick up the check, no questions asked.

Actually, our family's involvement in the restaurant business was a bit of serendipity and didn't come until a few years later, when Father and our older brother bought their own restaurant, Brennan's, in June 1946. Father was sixty at the time and bought the restaurant so he could retire and have an income, but he soon grew to love it. He died in 1958; probably the reason he survived so long was that he loved the restaurant business so much and adored working with the food. Eventually, as the restaurant started prospering, other members of the family fell in, until everyone was involved.

Learning about the restaurant business and about food was new and exciting then. We never minded the long hours, because it always seemed to us that if you had to work for a living, this was probably the nicest way to do it.

Paul Blangé, the chef at Brennan's, was another cook from whom we all learned a great deal about food. The restaurant was closed on Sundays, but the chefs would come in to keep the stockpots going. So we would go back Sunday mornings and sit with Paul and have breakfast and talk about food. He would fix a little something, often egg dishes, which is how the family grew so fond of eggs in all their many manifestations.

Paul Blangé got us so intrigued that we soon started spending every spare minute in the kitchen, watching the dishes being made, asking questions, tasting, smelling, and studying Escoffier like a textbook. Paul had two wonderful early-nineteenth-century cookbooks, which he kept wrapped in brown paper, with classic French recipes printed in English. They were a great revelation and a terrific resource. He gave them to the family when he retired, and we treasure them. From Paul we discovered this great big food world out there and centuries of accumulated knowledge, so we madly began studying and collecting cookbooks—to understand the history of food, the chemistry of certain combinations, and just for inspiration. Today when Ella travels to New York, she takes an empty suitcase just to bring back all the new cookbooks!

Even in those early days, we knew we wanted to change the traditional New Orleans restaurant menu and develop new dishes—to go beyond trout almondine and oysters Rockefeller.

Traveling was the next step in our education, and a great source of inspiration and culinary ideas. We visited restaurants all over the country, concentrating on New York and San Francisco, talked with owners and chefs, and tasted, of course. You might call it an "edible education." In those days, it was really the only way to learn, because we never went to culinary school. In New York, our favorite temples of taste were the "21" Club, Pavillon, and Café Chambord. There were certain people who were very important as mentors. Lucius Beebe, one of the original owners of *The New Yorker*, who wrote a column first there and then in *Gourmet*, was a very wealthy man and a bon vivant, who was most kind about teaching us and sending us to the right places. And we were always close to the "21" family, who have been wonderfully helpful and very good friends over the years.

Then we traveled to Europe, which was a broadening experience, because we were being exposed to things we had never seen before—new ingredients, stylized presentations, and a proud professionalism in the art of serving.

When we started at Brennan's we were the young upstarts on the New Orleans restaurant scene. We wanted to learn how to run a fine restaurant, and eventually we did establish ours as one of the top three restaurants in New Orleans.

It was breakfast that really put us on the map, not just locally but nationally. Our brother Owen said, "Dammit, if they can have 'Dinner at Antoine's,' we can have 'Breakfast at Brennan's'!" The idea was to do something exciting and new to get attention for the restaurant. When we traveled to New York, London, and Paris to research dishes, we discovered there wasn't any restaurant serving breakfast. So we took egg recipes from Chef Blangé's nineteenth-century cookbooks and adapted them to Creole tastes with local ingredients, added flaming desserts like crêpes Suzette for drama, and started the custom of drinking before breakfast. Owen said, "We need an 'eye-opener' to wake people up"; now it is traditional for customers to sit there by the hour drinking. The classic joke was that Ella had to sweep out the brunch crowd before the dinner guests arrived.

At Brennan's we were not only trying to keep up with the old established restaurants, we were trying to be ahead of them. We stayed open very late, serving dinner until midnight. We always tried to present dishes that were not exactly the same as the other restaurants. And Brennan's was the first restaurant in New Orleans that was decorated in a luxurious style, with rugs on the floors and candles on the tables. In 1955, when we moved to the building on Royal Street, it was absolutely gorgeous. We all worked there until 1973, at which time Owen's three sons were grown up and able to take on the responsibility of Brennan's themselves. So the five of us from the older generation—Dick, John, Ella, Adelaide, and Dottie (Owen had died)—eager for a new challenge, decided to start all over again and achieve elsewhere the success we had achieved at Brennan's. It was family teamwork that made Brennan's a New Orleans landmark, and today we are trying to create a similar success with Commander's Palace.

When Commander's Palace came on the market in 1969, we bought it immediately, not only because it was a beautiful Victorian mansion, but because it was in the historic Garden District, just three blocks from the two big old white houses in which we lived.

Built by Emile Commander in 1880, Commander's Palace had been a New Orleans landmark and a renowned restaurant for over a hundred years. Dick used to describe it irreverently as "the dead center of the Garden District," since it is right across the street from one of the city's curious old walled cemeteries.

The Garden District is the section of New Orleans that most resembles a romantic dream of the Old South. Stately Greek-Revival mansions with broad galleries, Corinthian columns, and lacy grillwork line the streets under moss-hung oaks and magnolias. Beginning as an exclusive suburb where wealthy Americans settled after the Louisiana Purchase in 1803, the Garden District is still New Orleans' most prestigious residential address. The grand homes and antebellum mansions, many inhabited by fourth- and fifth-generation descendants, are still the settings for lavish parties and balls, and remind visitors of scenes from *Gone With the Wind.*

Each Carnival, beautiful debutantes are presented there in a romantic ritual, to a world that seems timeless.

When we first saw Commander's, we were completely won over by its period charm, its fabulous fantasylike Victorian architecture replete with columns, turrets, and delicate, lacy gingerbread trim, and its lush green garden and picturesque patio.

Prior to our purchase, Commander's had had three owners: Emile Commander sold it to the Giarrantano family in the early 1920s, who sold it to Frank and Elinor Moran in 1944. They sold it to us in 1969.

Under Emile Commander, the restaurant enjoyed a superlative reputation for fine dining. However, during the Prohibition era of the early 1920s, under different ownership, Commander's took on a spicier reputation. While its downstairs dining room remained properly respectable for family meals after church, upstairs—entered by a secret side door—riverboat captains and sporting gentlemen entertained their lovely ladies of the hour. When we lived in that neighborhood as children, Mother used to admonish us: "Now don't you go in that restaurant." How ironic that seems now.

In 1944, when the Morans bought Commander's, adding the patio and gardens, its reputation returned to its former brilliant splendor. But after her husband died, Mrs. Moran had difficulty maintaining the restaurant.

As soon as we took over, we knew we wanted to give the old restaurant a new image, to put our stamp on it. The interior was dated, dark, and somewhat dreary, in Victorian decor with red flocked wallpaper and deep red carpets. We wanted to open it up, lighten the color scheme, and bring the airy outdoor-garden feeling inside—to bring the landmark up to date. We decided we needed something outside that announced "change!" The solution, which was somewhat controversial, was to paint the exterior of the building a vibrant turquoise blue, accentuated by contrasting white trim. It was the idea of a very dear friend and one of New Orleans' outstanding designers, Charles Gresham. We were afraid all the ladies of this subdued residential neighborhood would hate us, but Charlie said, "Don't worry, the color will fade beautifully." And it did.

Inside, Charlie and Adelaide transformed the dark Victorian decor, repainting and repapering with bright colors: yellow and green, white and peach. Outside, we replanted the garden with a green bower of palmetto, azalea, and bamboo. A magnolia and two cedar trees are presided over by an enormous oak, two hundred years old.

Upstairs, we replaced the outer wall facing the garden with glass to create the Garden Room. The result, which is very popular with our guests, is like eating in a giant treehouse, with vegetation and the ivy-laden limbs of ancient oaks pressing against the glass. Walls covered in white latticework, daffodil-yellow tablecloths, and grass-green carpet continue the outdoor effect.

A few years later, we created the Patio Room downstairs in the same style, with a glass wall looking onto the courtyard with its green foliage, exotic palm trees, and fountain. For six weeks in the spring and fall, we enjoy dining outdoors, and cocktails are served there all year round.

Downstairs, we kept the three intimate-scale rooms to create the feeling of dining in a fine private home. We saved the old mahogany moldings and Baccarat crystal chandeliers in the dining rooms, but pulled back the shutters to let in the sunlight and covered the walls in a light yellow linen fabric with a pale gray floral motif. The grill area, as you enter Commander's, is all mirrors and mahogany crowned with a huge antique brass chandelier that is so outrageously garish, it's grand. Legend says it was stolen by Jean Lafitte, the pirate who helped Andrew Jackson in the War of 1812.

One of the most unusual changes we made was to move the bar into the kitchen. Originally, it was to be just a service bar, but then it became an enormously popular gathering spot for guests. So when we renovated the kitchen, we moved the bar behind the kitchen and added a glass wall so you can still see what the chef is up to. To reach either the patio or the bar, guests have to walk through the kitchen. We have nothing to hide. The cooks love it, because they feel less isolated and more involved and can establish a direct rapport with guests. Having an open kitchen and communication with the chefs contributes to a relaxed atmosphere.

The Commander's experience becomes especially fun on Saturdays and Sundays at the Jazz Brunch, Dick's idea, when two outstanding live jazz bands and brightly colored balloons create a festive, party atmosphere.

The ambience we try to achieve at Commander's is one of casual elegance on an intimate scale. Visitors receive all the courtesies they would in our home. This is part of the Southern tradition of hospitality, and the way we were brought up to entertain.

The New Haute Creole

Building Commander's Palace is a twenty-four-hour-a-day proposition, a constant challenge. Most exciting has been our experimentation with a new Creole cuisine, which we call "Haute Creole."

New Orleans has had a colorful history. Its bustling port city was settled by the French in 1718, turned over to the Spanish in 1762, returned to the French in 1800, and then became American in 1803 with the Louisiana Purchase. En route, a few Germans, Italians, and Irish also immigrated to New Orleans.

Introduction

Classic New Orleans cooking, which is one of the most distinctive regional cuisines in America, originated with the Creole and Cajun cooks who took French cooking techniques and traditional recipes and adapted them to the new seasonings and ingredients they were introduced to by the local Spanish, Indian, and African population.

Creole is the French term for the Spanish *criollo*, designating descendants of Spanish or French ancestry born in the colonies. *Cajuns* refers to the French-speaking refugees who fled from Acadia in Nova Scotia after 1755, when the British vanquished the French in Canada. The Acadians refused to swear allegiance to the British and were forced to leave, finally settling in the bayou country southwest of New Orleans; they were ancestors of people now known as Cajuns.

There is some controversy about defining the distinction between Creole versus Cajun cuisine. Generally, Creole is closer to classic French cuisine with delicate blends and subtle sauces. It is a hybrid cuisine based on French traditions and techniques that gradually incorporated local ethnic influences and indigenous ingredients to create a unique New Orleans style of cooking. Cajun, on the other hand, derives from a more rustic style of cooking, usually in one large pot with spicier seasoning. Another distinction is that Creole cuisine takes more care with presentation than the more country-style Cajun cooking.

The French contributed an essential flair for cooking techniques as well as traditional provincial recipes (as distinct from *haute cuisine*); for instance, daube glacé, bouillabaisse, fish poached in court-bouillon, and the kind of savory soups that thrifty country cooks make from leftovers. The Spanish contributed their gusto for piquancy, the seeds of the hot red cayenne peppers, and their use of rice—abundant in Louisiana. From the Choctaw Indians the French learned about local herbs and spices and about filé powder, aromatic dried sassafras leaves pulverized in wooden mortars. Slaves from Africa introduced their slow-cooking methods and brought seeds from their native *gombo* plant, which flourished in Louisiana as okra. Hence, New Orleans gumbo, which uses okra as a thickener, got its name.

As a port city, New Orleans enriched its culinary repertoire from trade with the West Indies, Cuba, and Mexico, whence came sugarcane, bitters, tropical fruits and vegetables, new herbs and spices. Each influx of immigrants made its contribution, though the dominating influence was frankly French.

In classic Creole cuisine, the "Holy Trinity" was chopped celery, onion, and green bell pepper. Special seasonings, rich stocks, and sauces were the sine qua non of the Creole cook.

The unique Creole taste is a kind of wonderful "pow" flavor that explodes on your tongue like a Fourth of July fireworks display. Paul

Prudhomme, the talented Cajun chef we were lucky enough to have at Commander's for five years, describes the intoxicating power of Creole cuisine, in which "every bite is as exciting as every other bite, where all your taste buds are affected by turns—sweet and sour, salty and bitter—where the flavors dance in your mouth and shout hooray!"

When the first French settlers came to New Orleans, located ninety miles up the Mississippi River on the Gulf Coast and built mainly on marshlands, they adapted their recipes to take advantage of the plentiful local natural resources. New Orleans' strength is its seafood. Indigenous specialties include soft-shell, buster, and blue-claw crabs; crawfish; Gulf shrimp; oysters; turtle; redfish; pompano; red snapper; speckled trout; and flounder. Wild game such as duck, quail, squab, and rabbit are also available in season. And fruits and vegetables from local farms are bountiful, such as okra, mirliton, eggplants, yams, and Creole tomatoes.

Classic New Orleans fare comprises gumbos, jambalayas, and bisques, as well as some Louisiana specialties such as Creole cream cheese, deviled crab cakes, grits, red beans and rice, dramatic flaming desserts, pralines, and our famous chicory-flavored coffee.

But today at Commander's Palace there is a quiet revolution going on. The new Haute Creole is our attempt to reinterpret and refine classic Creole cuisine for contemporary tastes. The new Haute Creole is different from classic Creole in several important ways. Dishes are lighter and generally less caloric. We have taken the roux (a mixture of flour and butter or oil) out of gumbo, an almost heretical thing to do. We have cut down on the flour in sauces and created new light dishes such as oysters à la marinière in a delicate blend of oyster liquor reduction, white wine, and shallots. Our new version of the classic pompano en papillote, created by Ella's son Alex, is a fish fillet gently cooked in its own natural juices with fresh julienne of vegetables, served with a light hollandaise sauce on the side. We have added seafood soufflés to the menu, and they have achieved a surprising popularity among riverfront executives. Our soufflés differ from the classic French preparation in that the seafood is not completely puréed, leaving an interesting nubbly texture; and, of course, they are spiced with Creole seasonings. We are also offering more salads: fried chicken salad, cold duck salad, crawfish salad with stir-fried vegetables and pasta shells.

We use only fresh local ingredients whenever possible. If we can't get it fresh, it's not on the menu. This policy led to the transformation of trout almondine into trout with fresh roasted pecans and pecan butter, because the almonds were from California and the pecans grew in our backyard.

In Old Creole style, everything was cooked for hours—vegetables and meats were cooked to death. Now everything is being cooked to order *à la minute,* because we have better-quality ingredients. Vegetables and pastas are *al dente;* meats are lightly sautéed or grilled. For instance, the classic veal grillade was formerly made with inexpensive cuts of veal cooked in heavy tomato sauce; today our milk-fed veal is simply sautéed and served with a light Creole tomato sauce. One of our most popular fish, grilled (or blackened) redfish, is well seasoned with Creole spices and cooked on a very high heat for mere minutes. When ingredients are fresh, the less you do to them, the more flavor, vitamins, and food value you preserve.

We are also seasoning with less and less salt and more fresh herbs, for sodium-conscious customers. For instance, a delicate breast of chicken with tarragon has lots of seasoning and an intense herbal flavor. In making our stocks, we don't add salt because the bones have salt, which comes out in the cooking process.

Perhaps the most important innovation is in the reductions of stocks to intensify the flavor of our sauces. Stocks are not simple, but they are the key ingredient in a successful sauce. We actually simmer our duck stock for five days, continually adding more bones, to capture the very essence of the duck flavor.

New dishes are constantly suggested in the course of our travels. Oyster soup with dome pastry was inspired by a similar dramatic presentation at Paul Bocuse's in Lyon. We revived deviled crab cakes on our menu after being reminded how good they were while dining at Leon Lianides's Coach House Restaurant in New York City. We have also adapted nouvelle French and Chinese cooking techniques and Japanese modes of presentation. We have made a big effort to introduce our customers to native California wines and now sell about 80 percent California wines to 20 percent imported, whereas two years ago it was the reverse. We are also inspired by the burgeoning of small local producers to take advantage of our local Louisiana resources.

From its beginnings Creole cuisine has been experimental. It evolved with French settlers modifying their traditional Escoffier recipes to the produce of the New World. Based on adaptation and innovation, for centuries it has been a cuisine of instinct and intuition, with recipes often not written down, and no hard-and-fast rules. Sometimes there are as many different recipes for a dish (oysters Rockefeller, for instance) as there are cooks. So we are in one sense continuing the evolution of creative Creole cookery, bringing it into the twentieth century.

The development of Haute Creole is a slow and careful evolutionary process. This cookbook, Commander's Palace's first, is a record of where we are now. We look forward with enormous pleasure in the years ahead to more tasting and testing and refining of a classic American cuisine.

Drinks

New Orleans has been the city of civilized drinking for almost two centuries. Meeting and socializing over one of our famous frothy cocktails or a steamy café au lait is more than a tradition; it is a celebration of a way of life.

The American cocktail was, according to legend, born and named in New Orleans' Vieux Carré almost two hundred years ago. Folklore relates that in 1793, during the uprising of blacks in Santo Domingo, a young apothecary from a distinguished French family escaped to New Orleans, salvaging a secret family recipe for a liquid tonic compounded of bitters and brandy. The apothecary, Antoine Amadée Peychaud, soon opened a pharmacy at 437 Royal Street, where he dispensed his cure-all tonic over the counter to both the ailing and the thirsty. More to the point, Peychaud served his soothing spiced brandy in a unique way—pouring his potent potion into the larger side of a double-ended "egg cup," known in French as a *coquetier*, which through mispronunciation became *cock-tay*, and finally *cocktail*. Soon all New Orleans was imbibing his brandy cocktail, which differed from the usual brandy toddy by the addition of bitters. Thus the cocktail was born.

On plantations, where extravagantly luxurious entertaining was a way of life, drinks became very popular. The day often began with a breakfast tray holding an eye-opener of bourbon. Socializing—visits, fêtes, soirées, theatricals, parties, dinners—is still very important in New Orleans. The slow Southern pace means there is always time to enjoy a visit, to meet, relax, and chat over cocktails or coffee.

Daytime drinking originated in New Orleans with the merchants, who started work very early in the morning, so that their lunch was the main meal of the day, and drinking was a part of that. When we were children, many families had their main meal in the middle of the day, and wines and drinks were served midday.

When we began our Jazz Brunch at Commander's Palace, we thought it would be fun to revive the morning cocktail, so we scoured eighteenth- and nineteenth-century cookbooks, consulted history books, and talked to a lot of wonderful old folk. Among our most popular drinks on Sundays are the absinthe Suissesse, milk punch, and brandy flip.

When we first started the brunch, it was considered a little bit wicked to drink cocktails in the morning before breakfast, but now we have to sweep out breakfast customers at 5:00 P.M. to prepare for the dinner guests! The reason people can drink so much is that these are smooth morning drinks, often made with cream. Brunch has become a very popular way to entertain, and people really party.

At home, when we invite guests for Sunday brunch, we serve wonderful mixed cocktails before and strong black chicory-blended coffee after.

Chapter opening illustration: *As one of our bartenders mixes up traditional New Orleans–style cocktails, the chefs are busy in the kitchen.*

Absinthe Suissesse

MAKES 1 DRINK

Anything with absinthe is very much a part of New Orleans. A fashionable drink in nineteenth-century Paris among demimondaines, the green spirits were soon popular in New Orleans, especially at the Old Absinthe House on Bourbon Street. The absinthe Suissesse is a very old recipe that is perfect for a brunch. It has a lovely licorice taste and the smoothness of cream—perfect for the morning (or the morning after).

Since absinthe is forbidden in this country today, substitute Herbsaint or Pernod, which has the same licorice flavor. Orgeat syrup is almond-flavored simple syrup, available commercially.

- 1½ ounces Herbsaint or Pernod
- ½ ounce orgeat syrup
- 1 egg white
- ½ ounce cream or half-and-half
- 4 ounces shaved ice

Combine all ingredients in blender container, blend for 5 seconds, and pour into a chilled old-fashioned glass.

Brandy Flip

MAKES 1 DRINK

The flip was originally a hot drink served in a mug, much favored in America and England before tea and coffee were common. We revived an iced version of the brandy flip thirty years ago, when we started "Breakfast at Brennan's," and it is now very popular.

There are many variations made by substituting other spirits: rum flips, gin flips, whiskey flips, and yankee flips with apple brandy. Ella's favorite is the sherry flip.

Simple Syrup

- 1 cup water
- 2 cups sugar

- 1½ ounces brandy
- 1 raw egg
- Freshly grated nutmeg

1 ■ *Make simple syrup:* Combine water and sugar, bring to a boil, and simmer for 5 minutes. Let cool. Store extra simple syrup in a covered jar in the refrigerator for future use.

2 ■ Shake brandy, ½ ounce syrup, and egg in a cocktail shaker half filled with ice until mixture froths. Strain into a wineglass and top with nutmeg.

Sazerac Cocktail

MAKES 1 DRINK

This is the greatest morning drink in the whole world! The most famous of all old New Orleans drinks, the Sazerac cocktail originated in the Sazerac Bar in the Vieux Carré. This was an all-male bar, closed now, where men would go after work to do business—and drink. The cocktail is potent, and one is enough.

An impressive presentation, which our bartenders have perfected, is to coat the prechilled old-fashioned glass with Pernod by swirling it in the air and catching it. Don't try it out with your best crystal!

Herbsaint or Pernod
1½ ounces rye whiskey
⅓ ounce Simple Syrup (page 4)
4 dashes Peychaud bitters
2 dashes Angostura bitters

Garnish

Twist of lemon

1 Pour a little Herbsaint or Pernod into a 9-ounce glass. Roll glass between your palms until well coated. Pour out any excess.

2 Stir remaining ingredients with ice until very cold and strain into the prepared glass. Garnish rim with twist of lemon.

Planter's Punch

MAKES 1 DRINK

The Southern plantation owners' potent rum punch is perfect for lazy afternoons.

1½ ounces light rum
½ ounce grapefruit juice
½ ounce orange juice
⅓ ounce grenadine
½ ounce Myers's dark rum

Garnish

Slice of orange
Maraschino cherry

1 Fill a 12-ounce stemmed wineglass with ice cubes. Over the ice pour the light rum, fruit juices, and grenadine. Stir well.

2 Float the dark rum on top and garnish with orange slice and cherry. Serve with a straw.

Ojen Cocktail

MAKES 1 DRINK

Ojen is a Spanish absinthe with a subtle anise flavor, very different from the French. The Ojen cocktail is a delicious drink with a natural sweetness, and when you pour it over ice it becomes a delicate pale pink.

1½ ounces Ojen
2 to 3 dashes Peychaud bitters
Seltzer or soda water

1 In a mixing glass stir the Ojen and bitters with ice.

2 Add a splash of seltzer or soda water and strain into a 9-ounce old-fashioned glass.

Ojen Frappé

MAKES 1 DRINK

Ojen has such a delicate flavor, many people prefer it served neat and not mixed. But an elegant and simple aperitif would be Ojen served on crushed ice. It turns a pretty pink when put on ice and has a subtly sweet licorice taste. We like it before lunch.

1 ounce Ojen
⅓ ounce Simple Syrup (page 4)

Shake well in a mixing glass filled with crushed ice and serve in a 9-ounce old-fashioned glass.

Absinthe Frappé

MAKES 1 DRINK

A simple and easy absinthe drink that has many devotees. The ingredients are poured over cracked ice, stirred vigorously with a cocktail spoon, and then shaken for a few seconds. Serve in a tall thin chilled highball glass.

⅓ ounce Simple Syrup (page 4)

1½ ounces Herbsaint or Pernod

1 Fill a chilled highball glass with crushed ice and add the syrup and Herbsaint.

2 Stir vigorously until frost appears on sides of glass and serve.

Ramos Gin Fizz

MAKES 1 DRINK

One of New Orleans's most famous drinks, the Ramos gin fizz was named after Henry C. Ramos, who invented it in the 1880s in his bar at Meyer's Restaurant. The original recipe has always been a well-guarded secret. The thick, frothy mixture with its delicate bouquet of orange-flower water makes it one of our most popular brunch drinks, especially in spring and summer, when people love to sip it out on the patio.

If using an electric blender, mix the ingredients at high speed until thick and airy, then serve in tall thin glasses or double old-fashioned glasses.

1½ ounces gin
½ ounce Simple Syrup (page 4)
1 dash orange-flower water
1 egg white
⅓ ounce lemon juice
2 ounces half-and-half or light cream

1 Half fill a cocktail shaker with ice cubes. Add gin and remaining ingredients.

2 Shake until frothy and strain into a 9-ounce old-fashioned glass.

Sidecar Cocktail

MAKES 1 DRINK

The sidecar was once the smart drink of two continents. It was the inspiration for the Duke of Windsor's Cointreau drink that he named the "Wallis Blue" for his bride at their prenuptial dinner.

Folklore relates that it was originally created by accident when an innkeeper in France, upset by news of his sidecar's being damaged, mistakenly combined orders for brandy, Cointreau, and lemon juice in a single glass. The result found instant popularity.

Granulated sugar
1½ ounces brandy
½ ounce Triple Sec
1 ounce lemon juice

1 Rub the edge of a 9-ounce stemmed wineglass with an ice cube to moisten, and dip in sugar.

2 Pour remaining ingredients into a mixing glass filled with ice cubes and shake well.

3 Strain into the prepared glass.

Mint Julep

MAKES 1 DRINK

The julep was a traditional offering at the old plantations of the South. There are at least as many "authentic" mint julep recipes as there are Southern states. Common to them all is the requirement of fresh mint. The mint is put in the bottom of the glass with the sugar and is crushed with a muddler (a little wooden baton) to get the fresh mint essence. Served in a tall highball glass garnished with an extra sprig of mint, this refreshing drink is especially good in the summer for Saturday- or Sunday-afternoon socializing.

About 20 fresh mint leaves
⅓ ounce Simple Syrup (page 4)
½ ounce water
2 ounces 90- to 100-proof bourbon

Garnish

Sprig of mint
Brandy

1 ■ Put mint leaves in a 14-ounce glass or silver mug. Add syrup and water and crush leaves with a muddler.

2 ■ Fill glass with crushed ice and pour in the bourbon.

3 ■ Agitate with mixing spoon until outside of glass is coated with frost.

4 ■ Garnish with a sprig of mint and top with a splash of brandy.

Singapore Sling

MAKES 1 DRINK

In the old days, a drink was mixed by "slinging" it from one mug to another. Generally served in a tall thin "mint julep glass" with plenty of crushed ice, this makes a lovely afternoon drink.

1½ ounces gin
⅓ ounce Simple Syrup (page 4)
½ ounce seltzer or soda water
½ ounce cherry brandy
Juice of ½ lemon

Garnish

Slice of orange
Maraschino cherry

1 ■ Fill a 12-ounce stemmed wineglass with crushed ice. Pour gin and syrup over the ice and mix well.

2 ■ Add seltzer or soda water to almost fill the glass.

3 ■ Float cherry brandy on top and garnish with orange slice and cherry. Serve with a straw.

Negroni

MAKES 1 DRINK

Charles Gresham, a dear friend who helped us decorate Commander's Palace, first introduced us to the negroni cocktail in a small café on the Via Veneto in Italy. One of the most elegant Italian cocktails, it's a marvelously dry and light drink with a beautiful deep amber color reminiscent of their ancient frescoes.

½ ounce gin
½ ounce sweet vermouth
½ ounce Campari
Splash of seltzer or soda water

Garnish

Twist of lemon

1 Pour gin, vermouth, and Campari into a cocktail glass half filled with ice cubes.

2 Shake well and strain into a cocktail glass.

3 Add a splash of seltzer or soda water and garnish with a twist of lemon.

Milk Punch

MAKES 1 DRINK

The milk punch is really an American drink. Especially festive at Christmastime, this soothing drink is a pleasant tonic for the morning after, with milk and half-and-half and a delicate vanilla flavor. We love to mix it in a hand shaker until it's frothy and white, then add a touch of nutmeg on top for color.

1½ ounces bourbon or brandy
½ ounce vanilla extract
½ ounce Simple Syrup (page 4)
1 ounce half-and-half
2 ounces milk
Freshly grated nutmeg

1 Half fill a cocktail shaker with ice cubes. Add bourbon or brandy, vanilla extract, syrup, half-and-half, and milk.

2 Shake vigorously and strain into a 9-ounce old-fashioned glass.

3 Top with nutmeg.

Brandy Alexander

MAKES 1 DRINK

A luxurious combination of brandy, crème de cacao, and cream, a brandy Alexander tastes like a slightly naughty milk shake. The thick, silken texture and rich flavor make it a good substitute for dessert.

½ ounce dark crème de cacao
2 ounces cream or half-and-half
1½ ounces brandy
Freshly grated nutmeg

1 ■ Pour the crème de cacao, cream or half-and-half, and brandy into a cocktail shaker half filled with ice cubes. Shake.

2 ■ Strain into a 9-ounce stemmed wineglass.

3 ■ Sprinkle nutmeg on top.

Rickey

MAKES 1 DRINK

This popular cocktail is allegedly named for Colonel Joseph Rickey (rumored to have been a member of Congress). The quintessential ingredients in a rickey are freshly squeezed lime juice, then either vodka or dry gin, according to preference, and seltzer. The lime gives the rickey its wonderfully refreshing, slightly tart flavor—perfect for a sweltering summer afternoon, served in a tall glass with lots of clinking ice.

1½ ounces vodka or dry gin
Juice of ½ lime
Seltzer or soda water

1 ■ Pour the vodka or gin and lime juice over ice cubes in a 9-ounce tall highball glass.

2 ■ Fill to the top with seltzer or soda water.

Kir or Chablis Cassis

MAKES 1 DRINK

The Chablis cassis is the classic light French aperitif, and it is delicious. During the war years it was renamed kir, after the mayor of the town where they make cassis. He had been a war hero. Kir—either royale or Chablis cassis—is nice to serve before a particularly elegant dinner with wine when you don't wish to serve hard liquor.

⅓ ounce crème de cassis
Chilled Chablis

Pour the crème de cassis into a 9-ounce stemmed wineglass and fill with Chablis.

Kir Royale

MAKES 1 DRINK

The kir royale started with the French nouvelle chefs, people like Troisgros and Bocuse, as a variation on the kir. The addition of champagne makes it the most elegant aperitif. It's perfect to serve on special occasions, or just when you are in a festive mood.

⅓ ounce Chambord
Chilled champagne

Garnish

Twist of lemon

1 Pour the crème de cassis into a 9-ounce stemmed wineglass and fill with champagne.

2 Garnish with a twist of lemon.

Bloody Mary

MAKES 1 DRINK

Bloody Mary is, of course, the traditional morning drink par excellence, with improvisations limited only by the imagination. At Commander's Palace we add both Worcestershire sauce and Tabasco sauce to make it really spicy and give it a kick. At home, season to taste and, most important, use the best tomato juice you can find. We crush our own tomatoes to make juice when Creole tomatoes are in season.

½ ounce Worcestershire sauce
2 dashes Tabasco sauce
1½ ounces vodka
4 ounces tomato juice
Juice of ¼ lime

Garnish

Slice of lime

1 Fill an old-fashioned glass with ice cubes and Worcestershire sauce, Tabasco sauce, vodka, and tomato juice.

2 Squeeze in the lime juice.

3 Stir, garnish with lime slice, and serve.

Appetizers and Soups

Southern waters teem with an abundance of fish and shellfish of many varieties, and our cooks take advantage of this largesse in creating imaginative appetizers. Last year alone we used over fifteen thousand pounds of shrimp, not to mention wonderful oysters, crabs, crawfish, and turtles. We plan our weekly menus around whatever is fresh, in season, and readily available.

New Orleans is a soup town. In the old days, soup was traditionally the first course served at all dinners. From a hearty gumbo full of seafood and vegetables to a light and delicate consommé, soups are always soothing and soulful. We make bisques, gumbos, a delicate oyster broth, an aromatic Creole onion soup, and a variety of cream-based cold vegetable soups that are perfect for sultry Southern summers.

Gumbo (the African word for okra) is an original creation indigenous to the city of New Orleans, developed out of local ingredients: seafood, vegetables, okra or filé powder, and rice. Gumbo is a hearty dish, somewhere between a soup and a stew, and it can be used as either an appetizer or an entree. Gumbos are a particularly practical party dish for a large group when you're not sure how many guests are coming. In the Brennan family we like to serve gumbo after a football game or a political gathering. There are always two or three varieties, served with a large bowl of rice on the side and a wonderful fresh green salad. In 1803 a society banquet in New Orleans featured twenty-four different kinds of gumbo!

A gumbo can contain virtually anything, and it is said that no two are alike. There are those thickened with fresh okra and those thickened with filé powder, which is ground dried sassafras leaves originally discovered by the Choctaw Indians. Okra can be put in at the beginning and simmered along with the vegetables,

though it subtly alters the flavor. Filé powder must be added at the last minute, just before serving, or it may become gummy.

For hundreds of years, the traditional base of a gumbo was a roux: a mixture of flour and fat, such as butter or oil. One of the ways we decided to lighten this classic New Orleans soup was by taking the roux out of the gumbo. The gumbo is just as delicious, but more in the style of a French bouillabaisse. We have included recipes for our seafood gumbo as well as gumbo ya ya, which is a spicy Cajun dish made with andouille sausage.

Our appetizers, of course, also include such classic New Orleans dishes as shrimp rémoulade, crab meat ravigote, crêpe fruits de mer, vichyssoise, and Senegalese soup. But our new light favorites are oysters à la marinière, sweet and succulent oysters from nearby brackish waters, cooked in a simple reduction of oyster liquid, wine, and shallots; oyster soup with dome pastry, a delicate broth crowned by a pastry dome that emits a highly aromatic bouquet when cut; shrimp and mushroom sauté, enhanced by a light butter-and-wine sauce; shrimp soufflé and oyster soufflé; royale of leeks and mushrooms, a light custard with vegetables; crab meat and corn bisque; and cream of eggplant soup, one of Ella's personal favorites. Along with our appetizers and soups we always serve our popular garlic bread.

Chapter opening illustration: *The kitchen at Commander's Palace. Guests walk through the kitchen on their way to either the bar or the patio and get a chance to see what the chefs are up to.*

Commander's Garlic Bread

SERVES 6 TO 8

Our special Parmesan and dill-scented garlic bread is a great favorite with our customers. It's wonderful with almost any appetizer or soup. Make lots—it will disappear rapidly from the table!

- 1 loaf French bread, about 14 inches long
- 8 tablespoons (1 stick) unsalted butter
- 2 cloves of garlic, mashed to a purée
- ¼ cup finely chopped fresh dill
- ¼ cup freshly grated Parmesan cheese

1 ■ Preheat oven to 375°.

2 ■ Slice bread lengthwise. Melt butter in a small skillet, add garlic, and heat gently for 2 minutes.

3 ■ Brush the melted butter generously on the cut sides of the bread halves. Sprinkle with dill and cheese.

4 ■ Bake until golden and very hot, 5 to 8 minutes. Cut each half crosswise into 1-inch slices and serve immediately with appetizers or soups.

Commander's Shrimp Rémoulade

SERVES 10

An updated, lighter version of the classic rémoulade, our sauce is made with Zatarain's Creole mustard. If this is not available, you can substitute any coarse-grained Dijon mustard. Be careful not to overcook the shrimp, and do not put them in the refrigerator after they are cooked, as they will toughen. As an alternative to boiling, you can sauté the shrimp quickly with Creole Seafood Seasoning (page 190).

Rémoulade Sauce

(MAKES 2½ CUPS)

¼ cup Creole mustard
2 tablespoons paprika
1 teaspoon cayenne pepper
1 teaspoon salt
½ cup white vinegar
1 cup finely chopped green onions
Dash of Tabasco sauce
½ cup finely chopped celery
½ cup finely chopped parsley
½ cup ketchup
½ cup prepared yellow mustard
2 cloves of garlic, minced
3 eggs (at room temperature)
Juice of 1 lemon
1⅓ cups salad oil

80 medium shrimp, peeled and deveined (8 per person), approximately 2½ pounds

1 Put all ingredients for the sauce except the oil into blender container. Cover and mix at high speed until well blended.

2 Remove cover and gradually add the oil in a steady stream. Sauce will thicken to mayonnaise consistency. Chill.

3 Boil or sauté shrimp until done. Let come to room temperature. Serve topped with rémoulade sauce.

Shrimp Soufflé with Shrimp Sauce

SERVES 4

One of our newest and most popular appetizers, shrimp soufflé, is an elegant and light dish. It differs from the classic preparation in that the shrimp are not puréed but are left in rather large, ½-inch pieces for a more interesting texture and more intense flavor. The finished soufflé is not perfectly smooth on top, but golden brown with little soft mountains and cracks. It should be served in individual soufflé dishes with the accompanying creamy shrimp sauce.

- 4 tablespoons (½ stick) unsalted butter
- ½ teaspoon salt
- ½ teaspoon freshly ground black pepper
- 2 tablespoons minced celery
- 2 tablespoons finely chopped white onions
- 2 tablespoons finely chopped green onions
- 2 tablespoons minced green bell pepper
- 1½ cups small shrimp or coarsely chopped medium shrimp, peeled and deveined
- 2½ cups Shrimp or Fish Stock (page 191)
- 1½ cups all-purpose flour
- 4 egg yolks
- 6 egg whites

Shrimp Sauce

- 4 tablespoons (½ stick) unsalted butter
- 2 tablespoons all-purpose flour
- 2 tablespoons chopped green onions
- 1 cup small shrimp, peeled and deveined
- 1½ cups Seafood Stock (page 191) or half stock and half dry white wine
- ½ teaspoon dried thyme
- ¼ teaspoon minced garlic
- 1 cup heavy cream
- Salt and freshly ground black pepper to taste

1 Melt butter in a heavy saucepan over medium heat. Add salt, pepper, celery, onion, green onions, green bell pepper, and shrimp. Sauté, stirring frequently, until vegetables are tender, about 3 minutes. Add stock, bring to a boil, and simmer for 12 to 15 minutes. Add flour, ¼ cup at a time, beating with a wooden spoon after each addition until mixture begins to thicken and finally leaves sides of pan. Continue cooking and stirring for 5 minutes. Beat in egg yolks, one at a time, with a wooden spoon. Set aside to cool.

2 Preheat oven to 350°.

3 Whip egg whites at high speed until they form high stiff peaks. Fold about a quarter of the egg whites into the cooled soufflé base to thin it, then lightly fold the base into remaining beaten whites. Heap soufflé mixture into individual (8-ounce) buttered soufflé dishes. Bake for 15 minutes. Serve immediately, with the shrimp sauce served separately.

4 *To make the sauce:* Melt half the butter in a small saucepan. Add flour and cook, stirring, until mixture is smooth and bubbling. This is a blond roux. Set aside.

5 In a medium saucepan melt remaining butter and sauté green onions until soft. Stir in shrimp, stock, herbs, and garlic. Gradually stir in the roux, stirring after each addition until sauce is smooth. When all the roux has been incorporated, remove from heat, stir in cream, and correct seasoning with salt and pepper. Keep warm until ready to serve.

Shrimp and Mushroom Sauté

SERVES 6

A new and seductively simple dish, shrimp and mushroom sauté can be served all year round. As an appetizer, serve 3 or 4 large shrimp, for an entree 6 to 8, depending on size.

- 35 medium shrimp (about 1 pound)
- Creole Seafood Seasoning (page 190)
- All-purpose flour for dusting
- 8 tablespoons (1 stick) unsalted butter
- 1 cup finely diced onions
- 4 cloves of garlic, minced
- 1 tablespoon minced parsley
- 2 cups chopped fresh mushrooms
- 1 teaspoon Creole seafood seasoning
- 1 teaspoon all-purpose flour
- 1 cup dry white wine

1 Peel and devein shrimp. Sprinkle with seafood seasoning and barely dust with flour.

2 Melt butter in a hot sauté pan. Add shrimp, onions, garlic, parsley, mushrooms, and 1 teaspoon each seafood seasoning and flour. Gradually stir in wine and cook, stirring gently, until shrimp are done, about 3 to 5 minutes.

3 Serve on cooked rice or buttered toast points.

Note: Do not soak shrimp before cooking, as it leaches out flavor and color.

Shrimp Mousse

SERVES 6 TO 8

Ideal for entertaining, shrimp mousse is a delicate and decorative dish with a handsome presentation. Garnish with whole cooked shrimp encircling the unmolded mousse, and sprinkle a little freshly chopped tarragon or dill on top. It should be made a day ahead and chilled overnight. Do not leave it out of the refrigerator or it will liquefy.

- 1 pound shrimp
- 3 cups water
- 1½ tablespoons (envelopes) gelatin
- ¼ cup dry white wine
- ¼ cup dry sherry
- 1 teaspoon salt
- 2 tablespoons finely chopped tarragon
- ½ cup Homemade Mayonnaise (page 66)
- ½ cup heavy cream, whipped

Garnish

- Whole cooked shrimp
- Chopped tarragon or dill

1 ■ Peel and devein the shrimp and set aside. Put shells in a saucepan with the water and boil until liquid is reduced to 2 cups. Strain this shrimp stock and in it cook the shrimp until just tender, from 3 to 5 minutes, depending on size. Remove and reserve shrimp and continue to cook the stock until reduced to 1¼ cups.

2 ■ Soften the gelatin in white wine and sherry for 3 minutes, then add the hot shrimp stock and stir over low heat until gelatin is dissolved and stock is clear. Pour into a food processor or blender, add the shrimp, and process to a smooth purée.

3 ■ Chill the purée until slightly cool. Add salt and tarragon and mix well. Fold in mayonnaise, then whipped cream. Correct seasoning to taste. Spoon into a lightly oiled 4-cup mold and chill overnight.

4 ■ *To unmold:* Run a silver knife around inside edge of mold and invert the mold onto a chilled serving platter. Wrap mold in a towel wrung out in hot water until the mousse slips out of the mold.

Shrimp and Tomato Aspic

SERVES 6

This is generally served as a garnish on salads and cold plates such as charcuterie, pâtés, or assorted cold game. It is a pretty red color. Refrigerate until ready to serve.

- 1 quart Fish Stock (page 191)
- 2 tablespoons or envelopes plain gelatin
- 3 cups tomato juice
- 1 tomato, finely diced
- 3 green onions, finely sliced
- ½ teaspoon salt
- ¼ teaspoon cayenne pepper
- 18 medium shrimp, peeled, deveined, and cooked

1 Pour stock into a heavy saucepan and boil rapidly until reduced to 1 cup: This is a fish glaze.

2 Soften gelatin in tomato juice for 3 minutes, then add the glaze. Stir over low heat until mixture becomes hot to the touch and gelatin is completely dissolved. Remove from heat.

3 Combine diced tomato and green onions with salt and cayenne pepper and set aside.

4 Fill six 4-ounce cups or molds a third full with the gelatin mixture. Divide the tomato and green onions evenly in the cups. Arrange 3 whole shrimp in each cup and fill the rest of the way with gelatin mixture.

5 Chill for 4 to 6 hours or overnight in refrigerator.

6 *To serve:* Invert the cup or mold on the palm of your hand and run it under hot water. Shake and the aspic will slide out neatly.

Crêpes Fruits de Mer

SERVES 8 AS APPETIZER, 4 AS ENTREE

This is a centuries-old classic French recipe, which we decided to "Creolize" by using local seafood and special seasonings. Flaked crab meat or fish is added for textural contrast to the shrimp and oysters. Fill the crêpes generously with the seafood mixture, fold over to make half-moon shapes, and serve garnished with broiled tomatoes.

- 4 tablespoons (½ stick) unsalted butter
- ¼ cup all-purpose flour
- 2 cups Seafood Stock (page 191)
- 1 pound raw shrimp, peeled and deveined
- 4 cloves of garlic, minced
- 2 bay leaves
- 2 cups heavy cream
- 2 tablespoons paprika
- ½ cup dry sherry
- 1 cup coarsely chopped green onion tops
- 1 pound (2 cups) flaked lump crab meat, shells carefully removed, or nonoily fish
- 24 oysters
- Salt and freshly ground black pepper
- 8 Crêpes (page 164)

1 ■ Melt butter in a small saucepan. Stir in flour and cook the blond roux until smooth and bubbling. Set aside.

2 ■ In a 2-quart saucepan, bring the seafood stock to a boil. Add shrimp and return to the boil. Reduce heat and simmer until shrimp are cooked, approximately 5 minutes. Add garlic and bay leaves, and gradually stir in cream and paprika. Simmer for 3 or 4 minutes. Add roux and stir until sauce is smooth and thickened.

3 ■ Add sherry, green onions, crab meat, oysters, and salt and pepper to taste. Simmer another minute or so and remove from heat.

4 ■ *To serve:* Put 2 heaping tablespoons of the seafood-sauce mixture on one side of each crêpe, fold the other side over, and top with more seafood and sauce. Serve immediately.

■ ***Note:*** The crêpes can be made ahead and refrigerated, wrapped in a damp napkin to stay moist.

Oysters à la Marinière

SERVES 4

We love oysters but were tired of all those heavy sauces, so we took the basic concept of moules à la marinière and adapted it to oysters. This is one of Ella's personal favorites because it is so light and versatile. It could be used as an appetizer for an elegant dinner (allow 6 oysters per person) or as an entree for a special luncheon (12 oysters per person), accompanied by a green salad, French bread, and a bottle of fine dry white wine. It is imperative not to overcook the oysters. They should be merely warmed for 30 seconds.

- 24 fresh oysters
- 8 medium shallots, peeled and minced, or ½ cup minced shallots
- 1 cup finely chopped parsley
- ½ cup dry white wine
- ¼ teaspoon freshly ground black pepper
- 4 tablespoons (½ stick) butter
- 3 tablespoons all-purpose flour
- Salt (optional)

1 Shuck oysters, draining liquor into a bowl and dropping oysters into a shallow saucepan. Strain liquor to get rid of any sediment or shell and add ¼ cup to the oysters. Add shallots, parsley, wine, and pepper. Bring to a boil and simmer 1 minute.

2 Mash butter until soft and gradually mash and work in flour to make a smooth paste, or beurre manié. Add the beurre manié to the oyster liquid and stir gently over low heat until thoroughly blended, about 30 seconds. Correct seasoning with salt. (If oysters are salty it may not be necessary to add any.)

3 Serve as an appetizer in shallow gratin dishes, accompanied by sliced French bread or garlic bread to sop up the savory sauce.

Oyster Soufflé

SERVES 6 TO 8

One of our new seafood soufflés, similar to the shrimp soufflé. You can also make a mixed seafood soufflé with oysters, crab, and shrimp; so if you can't get one ingredient, you can substitute another. The texture will be a little looser than the shrimp soufflé, because oysters give up more liquid in cooking. All our seafood soufflés should be cooked and presented in individual soufflé dishes with the sauce on the side, and served with hot crusty French bread or our marvelous garlic bread.

- 4 tablespoons (½ stick) unsalted butter
- ½ teaspoon salt
- ½ teaspoon freshly ground black pepper
- 2 tablespoons minced celery
- 2 tablespoons finely chopped white onions
- 2 tablespoons finely chopped green onions
- 2 tablespoons minced green bell pepper
- 1 cup minced oysters
- 2½ cups oyster liquor*
- ½ pound (1 cup) freshly shucked oysters
- 1½ cups all-purpose flour
- 4 egg yolks
- 6 egg whites

Oyster Sauce

- 5 tablespoons unsalted butter
- 2 tablespoons all-purpose flour
- ⅛ cup chopped green onions
- ½ pound (1 cup) freshly shucked oysters
- 1½ cups oyster liquor
- ½ teaspoon thyme
- ½ teaspoon basil
- 1 clove of garlic, minced
- 1 cup heavy cream
- Salt and freshly ground black pepper to taste

1 Melt butter in heavy-bottomed saucepan over medium heat. Add celery, onion, green onions, green bell pepper, and minced oysters. Sauté until vegetables are tender. Add strained oyster liquor and whole oysters and simmer for 12 to 15 minutes.

2 With a wooden spoon beat in flour, ¼ cup at a time, and beat until mixture begins to thicken and leaves the sides of the pan. Continue to cook, stirring, for 5 minutes.

3 Preheat oven to 350°.

4 Beat in egg yolks, one at a time, beating after each addition until well blended. Set aside to cool. Whip egg whites at high speed until they form high stiff peaks.

* If there is not enough oyster liquor drained from the oysters, add water to oysters and liquor sufficient to make amount required. Drain oysters when liquid is needed.

5 Fold about a quarter of the egg whites thoroughly into the cooled soufflé base to thin it, then lightly fold the base into remaining beaten whites. Heap soufflé mixture into individual (8-ounce) buttered soufflé dishes and bake for 20 minutes. Serve immediately with oyster sauce.

6 *To make the sauce:* Melt 2 tablespoons of the butter in a small saucepan. Add flour and cook, stirring, until mixture is a smooth and bubbling blond roux. Set aside.

7 In a medium saucepan melt remaining butter and sauté green onions until soft. Add oysters, oyster liquor, herbs, and garlic, stirring gently. Gradually stir the roux into the mixture and simmer the sauce for 5 minutes. Remove from heat.

8 Stir in the cream, correct seasoning with salt and pepper, and keep warm.

Oyster and Crab Meat Ambrosia

SERVES 4

This is an old Creole dish combining deep-fried oysters and fresh crab meat in a very spicy seafood sauce. Make it only if you can get fresh crab meat.

- 1 quart oyster liquor (see footnote page 23)
- ½ quart red wine
- 3 cloves of garlic, chopped
- 1 cup sliced green onions
- ½ pound fresh mushrooms, sliced
- 1 cup Demi-glace (page 193)
- 1 pound crab meat
- ¾ cup all-purpose flour
- 1 tablespoon Creole Seafood Seasoning (page 190)
- 24 freshly shucked oysters

1 In a heavy saucepan reduce strained oyster liquor to 1 cup. Add wine, garlic, green onions, mushrooms, and demi-glace and over medium heat reduce to a thick smooth sauce.

2 Add crab meat and simmer over low heat for 2 to 3 minutes.

3 Mix flour and seafood seasoning. Dust oysters with seasoned flour and fry in oil heated to 350° until lightly browned, 2 to 3 minutes. Drain on absorbent paper.

4 Put 6 oysters on each heated serving plate and spoon some of the sauce over. Serve immediately.

Oysters Commander

SERVES 4

A delicate oyster dish, this is a new presentation and lighter adaptation of the traditional oyster-and-artichoke casserole. Place 1 oyster covered with oyster stuffing on each freshly cooked artichoke bottom. Ladle the oyster-artichoke sauce over and surround with 4 large outside artichoke leaves. The use of oysters and artichokes in both the base and the sauce creates a doubly intense flavor.

- 12 fresh artichokes
- 24 freshly shucked oysters
- 2 cups oyster liquor (see footnote page 23)
- 2 bay leaves
- ¼ teaspoon Creole Seafood Seasoning (page 190)

Oysters Commander Sauce

- 4 tablespoons (½ stick) unsalted butter
- 4 tablespoons all-purpose flour
- 2 cups coarsely chopped green onions
- Salt and freshly ground black pepper

Stuffing

- 4 tablespoons butter
- 4 tablespoons flour
- 40 freshly shucked oysters
- 1 medium onion, minced
- 2 cups coarsely chopped green onions
- 1 clove of garlic, minced
- 2 cups oyster liquor
- 2 bay leaves
- ¼ teaspoon Creole Seafood Seasoning (page 190)
- Salt and freshly ground black pepper to taste

1 Steam the artichokes until tender, 45 to 60 minutes, depending on size. Cool and remove the large outer leaves and the chokes. Reserve the bottoms, hearts (cut into quarters), and 16 most-perfect outer leaves.

2 Preheat oven to 425°.

3 Poach half the oysters in 2 cups strained oyster liquor with bay leaves and seafood seasoning until their edges curl. Remove with a slotted spoon and set aside.

4 *To make the sauce:* Reduce strained oyster liquor to 1½ cups. In a small saucepan make a blond roux: Melt the butter, add flour, and cook, stirring, until smooth and bubbling. Add to the oyster liquor and stir until well blended. Add green onions, one cup quartered artichoke hearts, and salt and pepper to taste. Return oysters to this sauce.

5 *To make the stuffing:* Melt the butter in a small saucepan, stir in flour, and cook, stirring, until the roux is smooth and bubbling. Set aside.

6 Grind the oysters in a food processor with onion, green onions, and garlic.

7 Bring oyster liquor to a boil and add the ground-oyster mixture, bay leaves, seafood seasoning, and salt and pepper. Simmer for 10 to 15 minutes.

8 Add the roux and cook, stirring, until well blended. Reduce heat and simmer on a low flame, stirring constantly, until mixture is very thick. Let cool, then refrigerate until ready to use.

9 *To serve:* Put 1 oyster on each artichoke bottom. Put stuffing in a pastry bag fitted with a large star tube and squeeze in a mound over each artichoke bottom and oyster. Arrange artichoke bottoms in a shallow baking pan and bake for 15 minutes. Ladle the sauce over it and garnish with large outside artichoke leaves.

Oysters Trufant

SERVES 6

An elegant and delicate dish, oysters Trufant are very lightly poached and served in a sauce of reduced oyster liquid and heavy cream. Oysters should be just warmed, not cooked, for less than 30 seconds. The sauce is also marvelous spooned over filet mignon.

- 1 quart heavy cream
- 5 dozen freshly shucked oysters, all liquor reserved
- 1 teaspoon Creole Seafood Seasoning (page 190)

Garnish

Chopped green onions or caviar

1 In a saucepan gently simmer cream and reserved strained oyster liquor until reduced to 1½ cups. This will take 2 to 3 hours.

2 Add 2 dozen of the oysters and cook for 5 minutes. Strain out oysters, leaving the sauce.

3 Put remaining oysters in a hot skillet with seasoning (no oil!) and toss gently to warm them. Do not overcook. Drain on towel, put on serving dish, and cover with sauce. Garnish with green onion or caviar.

Oysters Palace

SERVES 4

A hearty oyster dish with crab meat in a red wine sauce, this was originally an old Creole classic called oysters Jamie, which we made into an appetizer. It is also good as a main course, served with rice.

- 1 quart oyster liquor (see footnote page 23)
- 2 cups red wine
- 3 cloves of garlic, chopped
- 1 cup sliced green onions
- ½ pound fresh mushrooms, sliced
- 1 cup Demi-glace (page 193)
- 1 pound fresh crab meat
- 24 oysters
- 1 tablespoon butter

1 Reserve ¼ cup oyster liquor and pour the rest into a heavy saucepan and bring to a boil. Reduce over high heat to 1 cup. Add wine and continue cooking. Add garlic, green onions, mushrooms, and demi-glace, reduce heat to medium, and continue cooking until mixture becomes a rich, thick, smooth brown sauce. Add crab meat and simmer over low heat for 2 to 3 minutes longer.

2 Poach oysters in the reserved oyster liquor until edges curl. Add butter, stir gently, and remove from heat.

3 *To serve:* Arrange oysters on warm serving plates and top with the crab meat mixture.

Crawfish Mousse

SERVES 6 TO 8

One of our most delicate crawfish dishes, this is an excellent example of the new, light New Orleans cooking. The crawfish mousse is a pretty pinkish-red color with a fluffy texture—delicate, but well seasoned. Do not leave the mousse out too long before serving or it will liquefy. Serve with toast rounds or homemade melba toast (thinly sliced French bread dried out in the oven).

- 1½ tablespoons (envelopes) gelatin
- ¼ cup Fish Stock (page 191)
- 1 pound crawfish tail meat, cooked
- 3 tablespoons finely chopped parsley
- ½ cup dry white wine
- 1 teaspoon salt
- 1½ teaspoons Creole Seafood Seasoning (page 190)
- 1 tablespoon Worcestershire sauce
- ½ cup Homemade Mayonnaise (page 66)
- ½ cup heavy cream, whipped

1 ■ In small saucepan soften gelatin in cold fish stock for 3 minutes, then stir over high heat until liquid is clear and gelatin is dissolved.

2 ■ Combine the hot gelatin mixture with three quarters of the crawfish meat in a blender or food processor and blend to a smooth purée. Remove from container and refrigerate until slightly cool.

3 ■ Stir in remaining crawfish tails, parsley, wine, salt, seafood seasoning, and Worcestershire sauce. Mix well. Fold in mayonnaise and whipped cream. Correct seasoning if necessary.

4 ■ Spoon into a lightly oiled 4-cup mold and chill overnight.

5 ■ *To unmold:* Invert mold on chilled serving platter. Wrap mold in towels dipped in very hot water and wrung out. It will slip from the mold quite easily. Garnish as desired.

Crab Meat Ravigote

SERVES 4

This makes a light, simple luncheon salad when served on a bed of Bibb lettuce (garnished, perhaps, with a touch of caviar). For spring and summer it could be garnished with fresh fruits.

Toss the crab meat very lightly. If you overmix, the lumps of crab meat will fall apart, and you want them to be as large as possible. Try to use homemade mayonnaise for this recipe; it is more delicate and really worth the extra effort.

- ½ cup Homemade Mayonnaise (page 66)
- ½ cup Creole or Dijon mustard
- 1 teaspoon dry mustard
- Juice of ½ lemon
- 1 tablespoon Worcestershire sauce
- 1 teaspoon grated horseradish
- ¼ cup chopped parsley
- ½ cup capers, chopped
- 2 hard-cooked eggs, peeled and chopped
- 1 pound fresh lump crab meat, shells carefully removed

1 Combine mayonnaise, mustard, dry mustard, lemon juice, Worcestershire sauce, and horseradish.

2 Mix in parsley, capers, and hard-cooked eggs.

3 Add crab meat and toss very gently.

4 Serve, chilled, in crab shells or on a bed of Bibb lettuce.

Note: Creole mustard is available in specialty stores and groceries around the country.

Crab Meat à la Marinière

SERVES 4

This old New Orleans recipe is very different from oysters à la marinière, because it uses milk to make a very light sauce. Toss the crab meat gently, and bake in individual ramekins. (You can make one large casserole for four if you prefer.) Serve with rice, toast points, or French bread, and a little watercress for color.

- 8 tablespoons (1 stick) unsalted butter
- 1 cup finely chopped green onions
- 3 tablespoons all-purpose flour
- 2 cups milk
- ½ teaspoon salt
- ¼ teaspoon cayenne pepper
- ⅓ cup dry white wine
- 1 egg yolk, beaten
- 2 cups (1 pound) fresh lump crab meat, shells carefully removed
- Paprika

1 Preheat oven to 450°.

2 In a large skillet melt butter and sauté green onions until tender. Blend in flour and cook over low heat, stirring constantly, for 5 minutes. Add milk and stir until sauce is smooth. Stir in salt, cayenne pepper, and wine. Reduce heat and cook for 10 minutes, stirring occasionally.

3 Combine 1 cup of the sauce with the beaten egg yolk, then stir egg mixture into the sauce. Stir until well blended. Add crab meat and toss gently.

4 Spoon into individual casseroles and sprinkle lightly with paprika. Bake until light brown, 8 to 10 minutes.

Buster Crabs

SERVES 4

Buster crabs are crabs caught molting their shells. They are in season between April and August. If you don't have a deep-fat fryer you can fry them in a skillet with 1 inch of oil or shortening heated to 400°. These cannot be cooked ahead of time, but must be served immediately to retain the wonderful contrast of the crispy outside and juicy inside. Serve them with just a dollop of béarnaise sauce or choron sauce (one part béarnaise and one part Creole sauce) or with butter mashed with chopped tarragon or dill. They can also be served as a main course, on a bed of spinach sautéed in garlic and oil.

Blue Atlantic crabs molt in May, becoming the famous seasonal soft-shell crabs from Chesapeake Bay. These may be substituted for the Southern buster crabs.

- 16 small live buster crabs
- Creole Seafood Seasoning (page 190)
- All-purpose flour
- Oil for deep-frying
- 16 toast triangles
- 1 cup Béarnaise Sauce (page 196) or Choron Sauce (page 197)

1 Clean the crabs and remove the apron, lungs, and legs. If using soft-shell crabs, do not remove legs. Sprinkle with Creole seafood seasoning and dust with flour. Fry in deep oil heated to 350° until golden brown and crisp, 1 to 2 minutes. Drain on paper towel and serve on warmed plates, 4 crabs per plate, separated by toast points.

2 Spoon a generous dollop (¼ cup) of sauce on the side and serve immediately.

Escargots with Angel-Hair Pasta

SERVES 4 TO 6

This dish is a cross-cultural combination of French, Italian, and Creole tastes. In New Orleans angel-hair pasta has always been served with garlic and oil. We decided to mix it with French escargots, which traditionally are served in garlic butter. The Pernod makes this dish special and gives it a hint of anise. You can substitute vermicelli for angel hair if you wish. And if you have to buy a bottle of Pernod for this dish, serve Sazerac Cocktails (page 5) another evening before dinner.

- 2 quarts water
- 1 teaspoon salt
- ¾ pound angel-hair pasta
- 36 snails, out of shell
- ½ pound (2 sticks) unsalted butter
- 2 tablespoons minced garlic
- ¼ cup minced parsley
- 2 shallots, finely chopped
- 2 cups heavy cream
- ¼ cup Pernod
- 1 ounce dry white wine
- 1 tablespoon Creole Seafood Seasoning (page 190)
- Salt and freshly ground black pepper to taste

1 ■ Heat the water and salt in a 3- or 4-quart saucepan. When water boils add the pasta and cook *al dente*. Follow directions on package and be careful not to overcook. Drain, rinse, and keep warm.

2 ■ Sauté the snails in butter until hot, about 1 minute. Add garlic, parsley, and shallots. Stir well. Add cream, Pernod, wine, and seafood seasoning. Simmer, stirring, until sauce is reduced and is smooth and creamy, about 5 minutes longer.

3 ■ Season to taste and serve over the warm pasta in a casserole or on individual serving dishes.

Royale of Leeks and Mushrooms

SERVES 4 TO 6

This savory custard timbale of delicately flavored vegetables is a two-hundred-year-old classic Escoffier recipe, with just a touch more seasoning. It can be served as an appetizer or as a vegetable accompaniment to fish or veal.

- 2 large leeks, about 6 ounces each
- ½ pound fresh mushrooms, sliced
- 4 tablespoons (½ stick) unsalted butter
- Freshly ground black pepper
- 1 pint (2 cups) heavy cream
- 7 eggs
- Dash of salt
- Dash of nutmeg

1 Preheat oven to 300°.

2 Wash leeks, carefully rinsing out any sand between the layers. Discard tough green stalks and slice into short julienne strips.

3 Sauté leeks and mushrooms in butter until tender, about 5 minutes, and season well with pepper.

4 Butter individual 6-ounce charlotte molds or custard cups. Put the sautéed vegetables into the molds.

5 Whisk together cream and eggs until well blended. Season with salt and nutmeg. Pour into the molds, filling them to the top.

6 Set cups in a shallow pan of hot water and bake until custard is set, about 45 minutes. Unmold and serve immediately.

Crawfish Bisque

SERVES 8

The finished bisque will be a dark mahogany color, very rich and thick. It could be a meal in itself with a loaf of good bread. It is also excellent for a soup party, served with a fresh green salad, a toasty French baguette, and wine. Our family likes a red wine with crawfish bisque, such as a full-bodied Cabernet Sauvignon. Serve the bisque in a gumbo bowl: a wide flat dish a little deeper than a soup bowl.

The best and most authentic way to make crawfish bisque is to start with live crawfish, which must be purged and boiled, the meat removed from the tails and the fat from the heads. Our crawfish bisque is made this way. When you do not have sufficient time to do this, you can buy frozen crawfish meat, fat, and shells from Louisiana supermarkets and some fish markets around the country.

To purge live crawfish, put them in a large kettle or pot, cover with cool tap water, and add ½ cup salt per gallon. Let stand for 20 minutes. Change water, repeating the process. Drain.

Boiled Crawfish

- 6 quarts water
- ¼ onion
- 2 to 3 tablespoons liquid crab boil (a combination of herbs and spices, available in specialty food shops)
- ½ tablespoon cayenne pepper
- 10 pounds live purged crawfish (yielding 1½ to 2 pounds meat)

Crawfish Stock

(MAKES 2 QUARTS)

- Shells reserved from cooked crawfish
- 3 quarts water

Crawfish Head Stuffing

- 2 tablespoons (¼ stick) unsalted butter
- ½ cup finely chopped white onions
- ¼ cup finely chopped green onions
- ½ cup finely chopped green bell pepper
- ½ cup finely chopped celery
- 16 crawfish heads
- 2 cups crumbed corn bread
- 2 eggs
- Reserved fat from crawfish heads
- Flour for dredging
- Oil for pan-frying

Bisque

- ¾ cup oil
- 1 cup flour
- 1 cup finely chopped onions
- 1 cup finely chopped celery
- ¾ cup finely chopped green bell pepper
- 6 bay leaves
- ¼ cup Worcestershire sauce
- 2 teaspoons salt
- 1½ teaspoons freshly ground black pepper
- ¾ teaspoon garlic powder
- ½ teaspoon thyme
- ½ cup finely chopped green onion tops
- 1½ pounds cooked crawfish tails
- 1 cup chopped cooked crawfish tails
- 4 cups fluffy cooked rice

1 *To boil the crawfish:* Bring water to a boil with onion, crab boil, and cayenne pepper. Add crawfish, cover, and boil rapidly for 11 minutes. Drain.

2 While crawfish are still warm, break off tails where tail and body or "head" meet. You will see a little light yellow-orange fat at the top of the tail. Remove it and set it aside to add to the stuffing. Break the body apart —insert your thumb inside the cavity, above the leg and stomach sections, and pull down. Remove the fat thus exposed and set aside. Peel the shells from the tail. Save the shells for stock and set aside the tail meat. Set aside 16 heads for stuffing (2 per person) and add the rest to the shells for stock.

3 *To make stock:* Grind or chop shells coarsely and cover with water. Bring to a boil, lower heat, and simmer until liquid is reduced to 2 quarts. Strain.

4 *To stuff the heads:* Melt butter in a 9-inch skillet and sauté onions, green onions, green bell pepper, and celery until onions are transparent and vegetables are soft. Grind enough of the reserved tail meat to make ¾ cup, add to skillet, and sauté for 10 minutes. Remove meat from heads and combine with corn bread crumbs, eggs, and the reserved crawfish head fat. Mix thoroughly. Stuffing should be moist enough so that a small amount squeezed in the palm of your hand will hold together. If it is too dry, add a little milk or stock. Fill the heads, dredge in flour, and pan-fry in a little oil until lightly browned on both sides.

5 *To make the bisque:* Heat oil in a heavy saucepan until very hot. Add flour and cook, stirring constantly, until the roux is a reddish-brown color. Add onions, celery, green peppers, bay leaves, and Worcestershire sauce. Stir constantly until well blended. Add the stock, salt, pepper, garlic powder, and thyme and bring to a boil. Simmer for 30 minutes.

6 Add the stuffed heads, green onion tops and whole and chopped crawfish tails, and heat thoroughly. Serve over hot rice.

Crab Meat and Corn Bisque

SERVES 8

Crab meat is very popular in New Orleans, and this bisque is a timeless specialty. It is best to make it when corn is at its peak. To prevent the lump crab meat from breaking into flakes, we add it at the last minute, after all the stirring is done. According to New Orleans folklore this is a soothing and surefire remedy for the lovelorn!

- ½ pound (2 sticks) unsalted butter
- 1 cup all-purpose flour
- 1 teaspoon liquid crab boil
- Kernels from 4 ears sweet corn
- 1½ cups light or heavy cream
- 1 pound fresh lump crabmeat, shells carefully removed
- Salt and freshly ground black pepper to taste
- 1½ cups finely chopped green onions

Crab Stock

(MAKES 1 QUART)

- Shells from 6 medium hard-shelled crabs
- 2 quarts water
- 2 medium onions, quartered

1 ■ *To make stock:* Drop shells into water and add onions. Bring to a boil and simmer over low heat until liquid is reduced to 1 quart. Strain and set aside.

2 ■ Melt butter in a 5-quart saucepan. Add flour and cook, stirring, until flour begins to stick to pan. Add stock and crab boil. Bring to a boil, stirring constantly, and simmer 15 minutes. Add corn and simmer for 15 minutes more. Pour in cream and stir well. Gently add crab meat.

3 ■ Remove from heat and let stand for 15 minutes for the flavors to blend.

4 ■ Reheat gently to serving temperature. Add salt and pepper to taste. Just before serving add green onions.

■ ***Note:*** To hold for serving or to reheat, use a double boiler.

Seafood Gumbo

SERVES 20 AS AN APPETIZER, 10 AS AN ENTREE

We use the traditional recipe for gumbo here, but it is not thick or heavy because the roux is omitted. The excellence of the gumbo will be determined by the quality of the seafood stock. Gumbo served with rice can be a whole meal and is especially good with our garlic bread.

- 3 cups diced onions
- 2 cups diced green bell pepper
- 6 medium tomatoes, diced
- 1 cup tomato purée
- 1½ teaspoons thyme
- 1½ tablespoons minced garlic
- 4 bay leaves
- ½ teaspoon salt
- ½ teaspoon freshly ground black pepper
- 1½ pounds fresh okra, chopped
- 2 quarts Seafood Stock (page 191)
- 60 medium shrimp (about 2 pounds), cooked, peeled, and deveined
- 24 freshly shucked oysters, drained
- 1 pound lump crab meat, shells carefully removed
- 2 tablespoons filé powder

1 Combine onions, peppers, tomatoes, and tomato purée in a heavy 8-quart pot or Dutch oven. Cook on medium heat for 10 minutes, stirring occasionally.

2 Add thyme, garlic, bay leaves, salt, and pepper, blend well, and simmer for 10 minutes.

3 Add okra. When okra is bright in color and is cooked but still crisp, add stock. Bring to a rapid, rolling boil, then lower heat. Add shrimp, oysters, and crab meat and simmer for 15 minutes longer.

4 Combine filé powder with 1 cup of the soup. Remove gumbo from heat and stir in the filé-soup mixture. Correct seasoning to taste.

Note: Do *not* use a cast-iron pot to cook this soup, as it will discolor the okra.

Gumbo Ya Ya

SERVES 8

A highly seasoned gumbo classically made with chicken and andouille sausage, gumbo ya ya is of Cajun origin. If andouille sausage is not available in your area, any spicy smoked sausage such as kielbasa may be substituted.

1 large roasting chicken (about 5 pounds), disjointed
Salt
Cayenne pepper
Powdered garlic
2½ cups flour
1 cup vegetable oil
2 cups coarsely chopped onions
1½ cups coarsely chopped celery
2 cups coarsely chopped green bell pepper
6 cups Chicken Stock (page 192)
1½ teaspoons minced fresh garlic
1 pound andouille sausage, finely diced
4 cups fluffy cooked rice

1 Cut chicken breasts in half crosswise. This will give you 10 pieces of chicken. Season with salt, cayenne pepper, and garlic and let stand at room temperature for 30 minutes.

2 Measure flour into a large paper bag. Add chicken pieces and shake until well coated. Remove chicken and reserve the flour.

3 In a large skillet brown the chicken in very hot oil, remove, and set aside. Stir oil remaining in skillet with a wire whisk to loosen all the lovely brown particles from bottom and sides of pan.

4 Whisk in 1 cup reserved flour and stir constantly until the mixture of oil and flour (the roux) becomes dark brown. Remove from heat and add onions, celery, and green bell pepper, stirring constantly so they do not burn. Transfer roux and vegetables to a large, heavy saucepan.

5 Add stock to roux and vegetables and bring to a boil, stirring. Lower heat to a quick simmer and add garlic, sausage, and chicken. Continue cooking until chicken is tender, 1¾ to 2 hours.

6 Adjust seasonings and serve in gumbo bowls over steamed white rice.

Escargot Soup

SERVES 6 TO 8

An elegant appetizer for a special dinner party, this is an original Black Forest recipe from German chef Gerhard Brill. You must have a good heavy stock, half beef and half chicken, and a good dry Chablis. The creamy flavorful soup is very rich but light, and a Pinot Noir wine would be fabulous with it.

- 8 tablespoons (1 stick) unsalted butter
- ¼ cup finely minced shallots
- 1½ tablespoons minced garlic
- ½ pound fresh mushrooms, chopped
- 1 cup dry white wine
- 1 cup Beef Stock (page 192)
- 1 cup Chicken Stock (page 192)
- 1 cup heavy cream
- 3½ ounces chopped cooked snails
- ¼ cup minced green onions
- 3 tablespoons chopped parsley
- 1 tablespoon all-purpose flour
- ¼ cup Pernod
- 3½ ounces whole cooked snails
- Salt and freshly ground black pepper

1 Heat half the butter in a heavy saucepan, add shallots, garlic, and mushrooms, and sauté for 2 minutes, stirring occasionally. Pour in wine and stocks and simmer, stirring, until smooth. Add cream, chopped snails, green onions, and parsley.

2 *To make beurre manié:* Mash remaining butter until creamy and gradually mash in the flour to make a smooth paste.

3 Blend tiny bits of the beurre manié into the soup, whisking with a wire whisk after each addition. Add the Pernod and let the soup mellow over low heat for 1 to 2 minutes. Do not boil.

4 Add whole snails and salt and pepper to taste.

Turtle Soup

SERVES 6

Commander's is famous for its turtle soup, which is considered a great delicacy. Years ago we used to have soft-shell turtle stew, but that animal is now an endangered species. We now use loggerhead and snapper turtles from our own bayou waters, which are more abundant. This soup is dark, thick, rich—a stew-type dish, filling enough to make a whole meal in itself.

- 1¼ cups (2½ sticks) unsalted butter
- ¾ cup all-purpose flour
- 1 pound turtle meat, cut into ½-inch cubes
- 1 cup minced celery (4 stalks)
- 1¼ cups minced onions (2 medium)
- 1½ teaspoons minced garlic
- 3 bay leaves
- 1 teaspoon oregano
- ½ teaspoon thyme
- ½ teaspoon freshly ground black pepper
- 1½ cups tomato purée
- 1 quart Beef Stock (page 192)
- Salt and freshly ground black pepper as needed
- ½ cup lemon juice
- 5 hard-cooked eggs, finely chopped
- 1 tablespoon minced parsley
- 6 teaspoons dry sherry

1 Melt 1 cup (2 sticks) butter in a heavy saucepan. Add flour and cook, stirring frequently, over medium heat until the roux is a light brown. Set aside.

2 In a 5-quart saucepan, melt remaining butter and add turtle meat. Cook over high heat until meat is brown. Add celery, onions, garlic, and seasonings, and cook until vegetables are transparent.

3 Add tomato purée, lower heat, and simmer for 10 minutes.

4 Add stock and simmer for 30 minutes.

5 Add roux and cook over low heat, stirring, until soup is smooth and thickened. Correct seasoning with salt and pepper to taste. Add lemon juice, eggs, and parsley.

6 Remove from heat and serve. At table add 1 teaspoon sherry to each soup plate.

Note: If turtle bones are available, add them to the beef bones in making stock.

Oyster Soup with Pastry Dome

SERVES 6

Delicate oyster broth has always been considered a very fine soup in New Orleans. This new presentation, with a glorious crown of golden pastry, was inspired by a similar presentation that we saw at Paul Bocuse's restaurant in Lyon, France. As you cut into the pastry crust, a fabulous bouquet bursts forth.

- 8 tablespoons (1 stick) unsalted butter
- ½ medium onion, finely chopped
- 1 stalk celery, finely chopped
- 2 cloves of garlic, minced
- 1 large bay leaf
- 2 green onions, finely chopped
- ½ cup all-purpose flour
- 5 cups oyster liquor (see footnote page 23)
- 2 tablespoons Worcestershire sauce
- 1 pint freshly shucked oysters
- Salt and freshly ground pepper
- 3 tablespoons finely chopped parsley
- 1 pound frozen puff pastry, defrosted but still cold

1 Melt butter and sauté onion, celery, garlic, bay leaf, and green onions until tender. Add flour and stir until mixture comes away from sides of pan. Cook over low heat for a few minutes.

2 Add oyster liquor and whisk until smooth. Add Worcestershire sauce and cook over low heat for 30 minutes.

3 Add oysters and salt and pepper to taste. Bring to a boil. Remove from heat and stir in parsley. Pour soup into 6 individual ovenproof bowls.

4 Preheat oven to 375°.

5 Roll out puff pastry thinly on a floured surface and cut into 6 rounds the same diameter as tops of soup bowls. Put 1 round on top of each serving of soup.

6 Bake until pastry is puffed and golden brown, about 20 minutes. Serve immediately.

Morel Soup

SERVES 4

We served this cream soup at Commander's once for the Confrérie des Chevaliers du Tastevin with Chablis Grand Crus—to great acclaim! Use fresh morels if possible, or dried, or any combination of fresh wild mushrooms you can find in local specialty stores.

- 8 tablespoons (1 stick) unsalted butter
- 4 shallots, finely chopped
- 1 small white onion, finely chopped
- 6 ounces fresh morels (or 1½ ounces dried)
- ¼ pound fresh cultivated mushrooms, chopped
- ½ cup Cognac
- ½ teaspoon freshly ground black pepper
- 2 cups Beef Stock (page 192)
- 2 cups Chicken Stock (page 192)
- 2 cups heavy cream, or to taste
- ¼ cup chopped parsley

1 Melt butter in a heavy saucepan. Add shallots, onion, morels, and mushrooms. Sauté for 2 minutes.

2 Add Cognac and pepper and simmer over low heat until alcohol is evaporated. Simmer until reduced by half.

3 Add stocks and bring to a boil. Remove from heat and stir in cream and parsley. Serve immediately.

Creole Onion Soup

SERVES 6 TO 8

Not a French onion soup; this is a creamed onion soup that has no cream in it. It is very simple to make, but you must use a good, sharp, well-aged Cheddar cheese to give the soup its special flavor.

- ½ pound (2 sticks) unsalted butter
- 3 medium onions, thinly sliced
- ½ cup all-purpose flour
- 2 quarts Chicken Stock (page 192)
- 1 small bay leaf
- 3 ounces Cheddar cheese, shredded
- ½ cup dry white wine
- Salt and freshly ground black pepper to taste

1 Melt butter in a large, heavy saucepan and sauté sliced onions briefly. Just before they become transparent, add flour and stir well.

2 Add stock, bay leaf, cheese, and wine. Stir over low heat until cheese is thoroughly melted, then simmer for about 15 minutes.

3 Correct seasoning with salt and pepper and serve immediately.

Cream of Artichoke Soup

SERVES 6 TO 8

Not for dieters, this pale jade-colored cream soup is incredibly and wonderfully rich. It is especially good garnished with pesto.

- 4 cooked fresh artichoke bottoms, thinly sliced
- 8 tablespoons (1 stick) unsalted butter
- ½ cup finely minced cooked onions
- 1 cup finely minced cooked celery
- 2¾ cups Chicken Stock (page 192)
- Salt, cayenne pepper, and black pepper to taste

Blond Roux

- ⅓ cup (⅔ stick) unsalted butter
- ⅓ cup all-purpose flour
- 2 cups heavy cream

1 Melt 8 tablespoons butter in a 3-quart saucepan. Add artichoke slices, onions, and celery. Cook, stirring, until well mixed and hot.

2 Stir in stock, salt, and cayenne and black pepper, and bring to a boil. Lower heat and simmer for 15 minutes.

3 Meanwhile, melt ⅓ cup butter in a small saucepan, add flour, and cook, stirring, until the roux is smooth and golden.

4 Add the roux to the simmering soup and simmer for 5 minutes longer.

5 Remove from heat and gradually stir in the cream. Serve immediately.

Cold Potato Soup (Vichyssoise)

SERVES 6

3 tablespoons butter
1 medium onion (about 4 ounces)
¾ pound leeks, white part only
1 quart Chicken Stock (page 192)
4 medium potatoes (2 pounds), peeled and diced
2 cups heavy cream
Salt
White pepper

Garnish

Chopped chives

1 ■ Melt butter and sauté onion and leeks until soft but not brown. If they begin to color, add a little stock. When tender, add the stock, bring to a boil, add potatoes, and cook until tender, about 20 minutes.

2 ■ Pour half at a time into blender container. Cover and blend until smooth.

3 ■ Chill in refrigerator, then stir in cream and season to taste with salt and pepper. Garnish each serving with chopped chives.

Cold Asparagus Soup

SERVES 6 TO 8

This and the following three cold, creamy blender soups are perfect for warm-weather entertaining in spring and summer. You can prepare them ahead for weekends and have them in the refrigerator for unexpected lunch or dinner guests. At Commander's Palace they are served with a dollop of pesto, for garnish and added flavor, made by grinding together garlic, fresh sweet basil leaves, Parmesan cheese, pine nuts, and olive oil. Make these cold soups only in season, with the freshest vegetables you can find, and garnish them with small snippets of fresh vegetables, such as asparagus tips and delicate sprigs of watercress.

2 tablespoons (¼ stick) unsalted butter
½ white onion, diced
2 green onions, sliced
4 cups Chicken Stock (page 192)
1 pound tender asparagus
2 cups heavy cream, or to taste
1 teaspoon salt
½ teaspoon freshly ground black pepper

1 ■ Melt butter in a skillet or shallow pan and sauté white and green onions until transparent.

2 ■ Add stock and bring to a boil.

3 Place asparagus stalks carefully into the stock and cook until fork-tender, 8 to 10 minutes.

4 Set aside 12 asparagus tips and put the rest of the asparagus with the stock in the container of an electric blender. Cover and blend until smooth. Chill asparagus purée until cold.

5 Stir in cream and salt and pepper to taste. Garnish each serving with 2 asparagus tips.

Cold Watercress Soup

SERVES 6

- 2 cups Homemade Mayonnaise (page 66)
- 2 cups sour cream
- 2 cups heavy cream
- 3 bunches watercress
- 1 teaspoon salt
- ½ teaspoon freshly ground black pepper

Put all ingredients in blender container. Cover and blend until smooth. Chill before serving. Garnish with a sprig of watercress.

Cold Avocado Soup

SERVES 6

- 4 ripe avocados, peeled, seeded, and sliced
- 2 cups heavy cream
- 2 cups sour cream
- 2 peeled shallots
- 2 green onions
- 1 cup Chicken Stock (page 192) or milk
- 1 teaspoon salt
- ½ teaspoon Tabasco sauce
- Juice of 1 lemon
- ½ teaspoon ground cumin

1 In two batches, put the ingredients in a blender container, cover, and blend until smooth.

2 Empty into a bowl and chill until ready to serve.

Cream of Eggplant Soup

SERVES 8

This is a very popular soup all year round, and is one of Ella's personal favorites. It is thicker than most soups, almost like a purée. The curry taste, while not prominent, is very important. The eggplant must be completely peeled at least ¼ inch from the skin, or it will be bitter.

- 4 tablespoons (½ stick) unsalted butter
- 1½ cups minced onions
- 1½ cups minced celery
- 1½ cups finely diced potatoes
- 2 large eggplants, peeled deeply and finely diced
- 1 teaspoon curry powder
- ½ teaspoon thyme
- ½ teaspoon sweet basil
- 1 quart Chicken Stock (page 192)
- 2 cups heavy cream
- Salt (optional)

1 ■ Melt butter in a 6- to 8-quart saucepan and sauté onions, celery, potatoes, and eggplants until soft, about 25 minutes. Add curry powder, thyme, and basil. Cook until ingredients begin to stick to bottom of pan.

2 ■ Add chicken stock and cook until soup begins to thicken, about 30 to 45 minutes.

3 ■ Remove from heat, add cream, and season with salt if needed. Serve immediately.

■ ***Note:*** To reheat, use a double boiler.

Creole Tomato Soup

SERVES 6

Another glorious summer soup, which we make only during Creole tomato season, which begins in June and runs for six to eight weeks. If you can't get Creole tomatoes, use the freshest vine-ripened tomatoes you can find, such as beefsteak tomatoes. This should have the consistency of gazpacho. Do not strain.

- 4 medium tomatoes, peeled
- 3 stalks celery, coarsely chopped
- ½ onion, thickly sliced
- 3 green onions, chopped
- 1½ cups tomato or V-8 Juice
- ¾ cup cold Chicken Stock (page 192)
- 1 teaspoon salt
- ½ teaspoon freshly ground black pepper
- 2 tablespoons chopped parsley

1 ■ Put all ingredients in blender container, cover, and blend until smooth.

2 ■ Chill until ready to serve.

Senegalese Soup

SERVES 6 TO 8

A delicious and different appetizer or first course for a summer luncheon is cold curried Senegalese soup. It's very spicy, and we suggest it only for those people who really like curry. This soup is perfect for summer weekend entertaining, because it can be made ahead and served very cold. For special occasions you can dress it up by garnishing it with cheese croutons or a dollop of pesto.

- 1 whole chicken breast, skinned, boned, and diced
- 5 cups Chicken Stock (page 192)
- ½ cup diced onions
- ½ cup diced celery
- 2 tablespoons curry powder
- 8 tablespoons (1 stick) unsalted butter
- ½ cup flour
- 2 cups heavy cream
- Salt and freshly ground black pepper

Garnish

Chopped green onion tops

1 Poach the chicken in the stock until tender, about 20 minutes. Remove and set aside. Reserve stock.

2 Sauté onion, celery, and curry in butter without letting it brown. When vegetables are tender, add flour, stirring over gentle heat. Gradually add the stock, strained out from poached chicken meat, and cook, stirring, until soup comes to a boil and is smooth and creamy. Add chicken meat, let cool, then chill.

3 When cold, stir in cream and salt and pepper to taste. Garnish each portion with chopped green onion tops.

Salads

Although Creoles have always been famous for their excellent salads—particularly seafood specialties, such as fresh shrimp or crab meat salads served for lunch—in the past salads played a secondary role in Creole cuisine. But today that is changing rapidly. At Commander's we are creating more and more salads with a greater variety of ingredients, combining fresh local greens with a delicious diversity of fresh vegetables, herbs, seafood, game, and pasta.

With the more health-conscious attitude toward eating that most people have today we have noticed customers asking more for salads as main dishes. People want gourmet fare not only to taste good but also to be good for them. In addition, the climate in New Orleans makes you want to eat something cold; salads are a cool comfort during our hot summer days.

We have several popular new entree salads: fried chicken salad spiced with a dash of garlic and glossed with a special honey-champagne dressing; marinated duck salad with hearts of palm, green beans, walnuts, and raspberries and/or blueberries; and a pasta salad of Italian inspiration, with linguine, red onion, Genoa salami, olives, and mushrooms, sauced in a garlic vinaigrette.

We also have some special side salads, such as endive and watercress sprinkled with walnuts and dressed with a heavenly French walnut oil; and Commander's salad, with mixed greens, crumbled bacon, grated Parmesan, hard-cooked eggs, and croutons. Typical of Creole cuisine is the special attention paid to the many tangy and piquant dressings that complement these salads.

Helpful rules for superb simple green salads are as follows:

1. Use the best local greens you can find—avoiding iceberg lettuce.
2. Rinse and dry greens thoroughly.
3. Wrap dry greens in a paper towel or dishcloth and refrigerate for at least 20 minutes to crisp them.
4. Do not cut lettuce with a knife, but rather tear it with your hands into bite-size pieces.
5. Prepare dressing half an hour to an hour ahead, to let the ingredients blend together.
6. Dress the salad just before serving, tossing gently so that each leaf is coated with, not swimming in, dressing.
7. Serve immediately in a chilled bowl or on well-chilled plates.

Salad combinations are endless, limited only by the availability of fresh ingredients and your imagination. Inspiration can come from wandering through your local vegetable market and picking out the ripest, most beautiful and colorful seasonal vegetables and fruits. The key to spectacular salads is to use the very freshest ingredients.

Chapter opening illustration: *The patio area of the restaurant is filled with lush vegetation, palm trees, a fountain, and a grand old oak tree.*

Commander's Salad

SERVES 4 AS SIDE DISH

Our most popular side salad, this is a colorful combination of mixed salad greens, crisp crumbled bacon, Parmesan cheese, hard-cooked eggs, and crunchy croutons, all tossed in our special Commander's dressing. Use the freshest seasonal salad greens—we use leaf lettuce, field lettuce, Bibb, romaine, oak leaf, endive, and watercress.

- 4 cups mixed salad greens
- 4 tablespoons crumbled crisp bacon
- 4 tablespoons freshly grated Parmesan cheese
- 1 cup croutons

Commander's Dressing

(MAKES 2 CUPS)

- 1½ cups salad oil
- 1 egg, at room temperature
- ⅓ teaspoon salt
- ½ teaspoon freshly cracked black peppercorns
- ¼ cup white vinegar
- 3 tablespoons minced onions

Garnish

- 2 hard-cooked eggs, halved

1 Wash and dry greens and tear into bite-size pieces. In a salad bowl combine greens, bacon, cheese, and croutons.

2 Put ½ cup oil and the remaining dressing ingredients in a blender. Cover and blend on low speed. Remove cover and gradually blend in remaining oil.

3 *To serve:* Pour 8 tablespoons dressing over salad and toss. Divide onto individual salad plates or into bowls, and garnish each serving with hard-cooked egg half.

Crab Meat and Avocado Salad

SERVES 4 AS SIDE DISH

A delicate and colorful combination of avocado, crab meat, hearts of palm, tomato, and green onions. Use only fresh lump crab meat. Choose ripe, unblemished avocados, and slice them just before serving so they don't have time to discolor.

Commander's French Dressing

(MAKES 2½ CUPS)

¾ cup olive oil
½ cup red wine vinegar
4 tablespoons red wine
1 small red onion, quartered
2 teaspoons cracked black peppercorns
4 anchovy fillets
3 cloves of garlic
¼ teaspoon dried tarragon
¼ teaspoon dried oregano
¼ teaspoon dried thyme
1 teaspoon Worcestershire sauce
Salt to taste
4 sprigs parsley

---

4 cups mixed salad greens, torn into bite-size pieces
4 tablespoons diced avocado
4 tablespoons coarsely chopped hearts of palm
4 tablespoons fresh lump crab meat, shells carefully removed

Garnish

Tomato wedges
Green onion "brushes"

1 Combine dressing ingredients in the container of an electric blender. Blend well.

2 Put greens in salad bowl. Add avocado, hearts of palm, and 8 tablespoons dressing. Toss lightly but thoroughly.

3 Pile on salad plates and top each with 2 teaspoons crab meat. Garnish with tomato wedges and green onions slivered and fanned to make "brushes."

Neptune Salad

SERVES 6 AS SIDE DISH

Inspired by the sea, Neptune salad combines glistening morsels of scallops, shrimp, and crab meat and a tarragon-scented mayonnaise. Arrange the Boston lettuce leaves in a decorative fan shape, alternating with leaves of red Italian radicchio for color if you wish, and garnish with tomato and watercress.

Tarragon-Shallot Mayonnaise

- Ingredients for Homemade Mayonnaise (page 66)
- 1 teaspoon dried tarragon or
- 1 tablespoon fresh tarragon leaves
- 1 shallot, peeled and chopped
- ¼ cup dry white wine

- ½ pound scallops, cleaned and sliced
- ½ pound medium shrimp, cooked, peeled, and deveined
- ½ pound lump crab meat, shells carefully removed

Garnish

- 2 fresh tomatoes, cut into wedges
- 6 sprigs watercress or parsley

1 ■ Make mayonnaise as directed and leave in blender container. In a small saucepan combine tarragon, shallot, and wine and cook until wine is reduced to about 1 tablespoon. Add mixture remaining in saucepan to mayonnaise in blender jar and blend at high speed for a few seconds.

2. ■ Combine the seafood thoroughly but gently with the mayonnaise. Divide onto salad plates lined with lettuce.

3 ■ Garnish each serving with tomato wedges and a sprig of watercress or parsley.

Fresh Lump Crab Meat Louis

SERVES 4 AS ENTREE

This fresh lump crab meat salad is a Creole classic. The Louis dressing, served on the side, is a creamy mayonnaise spiced with green onions, green pepper, and chili sauce. Simply put the crab meat in the center of the greens and garnish with fresh seasonal fruits and vegetables.

- 4 cups coarsely torn mixed salad greens
- 1 pound fresh lump crab meat, shells carefully removed
- Slices of cucumber, celery, carrots, pineapple, melon, berries, etc.—your choice

Commander's Louis Dressing

(MAKES 2 CUPS)

- ½ bunch green onions, coarsely chopped
- ½ green bell pepper, seeded and coarsely chopped
- ½ cup chili sauce
- ½ cup heavy cream
- ½ cup Homemade Mayonnaise (page 66)
- Salt and freshly ground black pepper to taste

1 Pile salad greens on chilled salad plates and top with crab meat. On side of each plate arrange fresh seasonal fruits and vegetables in an attractive pattern.

2 Put dressing ingredients in container of electric blender, cover, and blend until smooth. Serve separately from the salad.

Salade Fontaine

SERVES 4 AS SIDE DISH

This is a colorful vegetable salad composed of sliced green artichoke bottoms, ruby-red beets, and jade-colored zucchini on a bed of leafy lettuce, topped with a sprightly dill mayonnaise. If you prepare the artichoke bottoms ahead, keep them in water with lemon juice to prevent discoloring.

Dill Mayonnaise

- Ingredients for 1¼ cups Homemade Mayonnaise (page 66)
- 1 tablespoon chopped dill
- 2 tablespoons dry white wine

- 1 medium zucchini, thinly sliced
- 4 cooked beets, sliced
- 4 cooked artichoke bottoms (fresh or canned), sliced
- 4 large Boston lettuce leaves

Garnish

- 4 sprigs watercress

1 Make homemade mayonnaise as directed and leave in blender container. In a small saucepan cook dill and wine until liquid is reduced to almost nothing. Add mixture remaining in the pan to the mayonnaise and blend on high for a few seconds.

2 Layer vegetables on salad plates lined with Boston lettuce.

3 Top each serving with ¼ cup mayonnaise and garnish with a sprig of watercress.

Salade Châtelaine

SERVES 6 AS SIDE DISH

An old-favorite side dish, salade Châtelaine is a combination of crisp watercress, artichoke hearts, chopped pimiento, and hard-cooked eggs in Commander's tangy herbal dressing.

- 6 cups crisp watercress leaves, washed and trimmed
- 6 cooked artichoke hearts (fresh, canned, or frozen), sliced
- ¼ cup chopped pimiento
- 3 hard-cooked eggs, finely chopped
- 1¼ cups Commander's Dressing (page 52)

1 Layer ingredients on salad plates as follows: 1 cup watercress, 1 sliced artichoke bottom, ¾ tablespoon chopped pimiento, 1 tablespoon chopped egg.

2 Spoon 3 tablespoons dressing over each serving.

Salade Gourmande

SERVES 4 AS SIDE DISH

A Creole variation on Michel Guerard's nouvelle cuisine classic, our salade gourmande contains thinly sliced green beans, watercress, pâté, and artichoke bottoms, sprinkled with pecans—all in a rich creamy green onion dressing flavored with Creole mustard. This is an impressive first course for any important luncheon or dinner party. For perfection, use twig-thin French haricots verts, taking care to cook them so they are still slightly crisp. If you don't have the time to make pâté, substitute your favorite pâté or foie gras from the local gourmet shop. Serve with a chilled California Chardonnay or a full-bodied white Burgundy.

- 1 cup thinly sliced green beans or haricots verts, cooked until barely fork-tender
- 1 bunch watercress, washed and trimmed
- 4 cooked artichoke bottoms (fresh or canned), sliced

Creamy Green Onion Dressing

(MAKES 1½ CUPS)

- 1 egg
- 1 egg yolk
- 1⅛ cups salad oil
- ¼ teaspoon salt
- ¼ teaspoon white pepper
- 3 tablespoons chopped green onions
- 1½ tablespoons Creole or Dijon mustard

- 4 slices pâté
- Watercress for serving
- 4 tablespoons coarsely chopped pecans

1 Prepare vegetables and set aside.

2 Put egg, egg yolk, and ¼ cup of the salad oil in blender container with salt and pepper. Cover and blend at low speed. Immediately remove cover and gradually add salad oil in a steady stream. Mixture will be thick and creamy. Add green onions and mustard and blend at high speed until thoroughly combined.

3 Put a slice of pâté on each salad plate. Beside it put ¼ cup green beans on a bed of watercress. Put 1 sliced artichoke bottom beside the green beans and sprinkle everything with pecans.

4 Moisten salad with a little dressing and pass remaining dressing separately.

Commander's Marinated Vegetable Salad

SERVES 4 AS SIDE DISH

Our special marinated vegetable salad includes a colorful combination of mushrooms, zucchini, red onions or celery, pimientos, and green beans, all flavored with a lively garlic vinaigrette. For best results, the garlic oil for the dressing should be made at least three days ahead. If you don't know exactly when you will need it, the oil and garlic may be stored in a sealed bottle in a cool, dark place for future use. It would be complemented by a light, dry Italian white wine or a spicy Gewürztraminer.

Garlic Oil

(MAKES 1 QUART)

- 4 tablespoons minced garlic
- 1 quart olive oil

Chapon Dressing

(MAKES ½ CUP)

- 6 tablespoons garlic oil
- 2 tablespoons red wine vinegar
- ¼ teaspoon dry mustard
- Salt and freshly ground black pepper to taste

- 1 cup sliced fresh mushrooms
- 1 cup fine julienne of crisp zucchini
- ½ cup diced red onions or celery
- ½ cup diced pimientos
- 1 cup thinly sliced green beans or haricots verts, blanched until barely tender
- 2 cups shredded Boston lettuce

Garnish

- 4 Enoki mushrooms

1 *To make garlic oil:* Several days beforehand, combine garlic and olive oil. Seal jar tightly. After three or more days, strain out the garlic and store in tightly closed bottle for future use.

2 Combine dressing ingredients.

3 In a mixing bowl combine all vegetables except lettuce and add dressing. Marinate in refrigerator for at least 2 hours.

4 *To serve:* Spread ½ cup shredded lettuce on each salad plate and top with 1 cup of marinated vegetables. Garnish with 1 enoki mushroom and serve with additional red wine vinegar and garlic oil.

Brennan Salad

SERVES 4 AS SIDE DISH

Another healthful vegetable dish, our Brennan salad includes avocado, artichoke bottoms, mushrooms, beets, and snow peas. The dressing is best made with fresh herbs, but dried herbs can be substituted if necessary. Line each salad plate with lettuce, arrange the vegetables decoratively, and finish with the herb-scented vinaigrette.

- Boston lettuce or romaine leaves, washed and dried
- 2 avocados, peeled and sliced
- 4 cooked artichoke bottoms (fresh or canned), sliced
- 1 cup sliced fresh mushrooms
- 4 cooked beets, sliced
- ¼ pound snow peas, blanched in boiling water for 2 minutes

Herb Dressing

(MAKES 2½ CUPS)

- 2 cups olive oil
- 4 anchovy fillets
- 3 shallots, peeled
- 1 teaspoon chopped fresh dill or ¼ teaspoon dried
- 1 teaspoon chopped fresh basil or ¼ teaspoon dried
- 1 teaspoon chopped fresh thyme or ¼ teaspoon dried
- 1 teaspoon chopped fresh oregano or ¼ teaspoon dried
- ½ teaspoon freshly ground black pepper
- ¼ cup white wine vinegar
- Juice of 2 lemons
- ½ teaspoon salt
- ¼ cup roasted whole pine nuts

1 Prepare vegetables and refrigerate until ready to serve.

2 Put all dressing ingredients except pine nuts in blender container and blend at low speed until well mixed. Pour into a jar and add pine nuts.

3 Line salad plates with lettuce leaves. On each arrange half an avocado, an artichoke bottom, ¼ cup mushrooms, a sliced beet, and a quarter of the snow peas. Moisten with a little dressing and serve more dressing separately.

Commander's Endive and Walnut Salad

SERVES 8 AS SIDE DISH

Perhaps our most simple and elegant salad, perfect for that important dinner, is endive and watercress tossed in a rich walnut oil dressing and sprinkled with crunchy chopped walnuts for added appeal.

- 4 Belgian endives
- 2 bunches watercress, trimmed
- ½ cup walnut halves

Walnut Dressing

(MAKES 2 CUPS)

- 1 cup French walnut oil
- Juice of 3 lemons
- ¼ cup chopped walnuts
- ½ teaspoon freshly ground black pepper
- 1 teaspoon chopped fresh dill or ¼ teaspoon dried
- 1 teaspoon chopped fresh tarragon or ¼ teaspoon dried
- 1 teaspoon chopped fresh parsley
- ¼ teaspoon salt
- 3 tablespoons red wine vinegar

1 ■ Trim and wash endives and watercress. Slice endives lengthwise into thin slivers and mix with watercress and walnut halves.

2 ■ Measure dressing ingredients into container of an electric blender and blend on low speed for about 1 minute.

3 ■ Pour enough dressing over the salad to just barely moisten, tossing gently but well. Serve on salad plates and pass remaining dressing separately.

Pasta Salad

SERVES 4 AS ENTREE

This new addition to our luncheon repertoire is of Italian inspiration. A cold pasta salad of linguine, salami, red onion, black olives, pickled mushrooms, and sliced cucumber is tossed with a spicy garlic vinaigrette and garnished with tomato and basil. It is ideal for summer weekend entertaining—everything can be made ahead and refrigerated for a last-minute luncheon party.

Garlic Vinaigrette Dressing

(MAKES 2 CUPS)

- 1 tablespoon minced pimiento
- 2 teaspoons drained minced capers
- 2 teaspoons dill pickle relish
- 1 clove of garlic, minced
- ½ small white onion, minced
- 1 tablespoon minced green onion tops
- ¾ cup olive oil
- ½ cup red wine vinegar
- ¼ cup red wine
- 1 teaspoon fresh thyme or ¼ teaspoon dried
- 1 teaspoon fresh oregano or ¼ teaspoon dried
- 1 teaspoon freshly ground black pepper
- Salt to taste

- 4 portions cooked linguine, rinsed and cooled
- Boston lettuce
- 1 red onion, sliced
- 8 slices Genoa salami
- 12 black olives
- 12 pickled mushrooms
- ½ cucumber, thinly sliced

Garnish

- Cherry tomatoes
- Sweet basil sprigs

1 *To make the dressing:* Mix pimiento, capers, relish, garlic, white onion, and green onion tops and set aside. Put remaining dressing ingredients in blender container, cover, and blend for 5 to 10 seconds. Pour over the pimiento-caper mixture and stir well. Refrigerate until ready to serve.

2 Put linguine on a bed of Boston lettuce on each plate and arrange on top the red onion, salami, olives, mushrooms, and cucumber.

3 Spoon 2 tablespoons of dressing over each serving. Garnish with cherry tomatoes and basil and serve remaining dressing separately.

Shrimp Salad I

SERVES 4 AS ENTREE

A very simple fresh seafood salad, this dish can be used as either an appetizer or a luncheon entree. It combines whole shrimp, celery, and green onions in a tangy rémoulade dressing. Do not soak the shrimp in water or put them in ice, because this will bleed the color and flavor. Arrange a fan-shaped bed of greens such as Bibb lettuce on each plate, put the shrimp salad in the center, and garnish with fresh vegetables such as sliced tomato, carrots, or blanched green beans or broccoli. As an alternative, the shrimp salad can be used to stuff avocado halves.

- 48 shrimp, cooked, peeled, and deveined
- 1 cup coarsely chopped celery
- ½ cup finely chopped green onions

Rémoulade Sauce

(MAKES 2½ CUPS)

- ¼ cup Creole or Dijon mustard
- 2 tablespoons paprika
- 1 teaspoon cayenne pepper
- 1 teaspoon salt
- ½ cup cider vinegar
- 1 cup finely chopped green onions
- Dash of Tabasco sauce
- ½ cup finely chopped celery
- ½ cup finely chopped parsley
- ¼ cup ketchup
- ¼ cup prepared yellow mustard
- 2 cloves of garlic, minced
- 3 eggs, at room temperature
- 1⅓ cups salad oil

- 1 cup Commander's Dressing (page 52)
- Bibb, leaf, or romaine lettuce leaves

1 In a mixing bowl combine shrimp, celery, and green onions.

2 *To make the sauce:* Put all sauce ingredients except oil in container of blender. Cover and blend at low speed. While blending, remove cover and gradually pour in the oil in a steady stream. Sauce will thicken.

3 Mix together Commander's dressing and 1 cup rémoulade sauce and pour over shrimp. Toss well and serve on salad plates lined with lettuce leaves.

Shrimp Salad II

SERVES 4 AS ENTREE

This is a delicious alternative to shrimp rémoulade. It is also wonderful with fresh lump crab meat.

Ravigote Sauce

(MAKES 2 CUPS)

- ¼ cup finely chopped parsley
- 4 ounces (½ cup) finely chopped drained capers
- ¼ cup Homemade Mayonnaise (page 66)
- 5 ounces (10 tablespoons) Creole or Dijon mustard
- 1 teaspoon dry mustard
- Juice of ½ lemon
- 1 tablespoon Worcestershire sauce
- 1 teaspoon prepared cream-style horseradish
- Salt and freshly ground black pepper to taste
- 2 hard-cooked eggs, coarsely chopped

- 48 medium shrimp, cooked, peeled, and deveined

Garnish

- 4 leaves lettuce

1 *To make ravigote sauce:* Mix together the parsley, capers, mayonnaise, Creole mustard, dry mustard, lemon juice, Worcestershire sauce, and horseradish. Season to taste with salt and pepper. Carefully fold in the eggs.

2 Mix shrimp with the sauce and pile onto salad plates.

3 Garnish with lettuce leaves.

Duck Salad

SERVES 6 AS ENTREE

This is a marvelous way to use leftover roast duck. The cubed duck meat is marinated for twenty-four hours in a honeyed French vinaigrette dressing and served on a bed of salad greens with a decorative array of fresh vegetables, fruits, and walnuts. We use crisp green beans and sliced hearts of palm, along with fresh raspberries and/or blueberries for color. You can improvise with a variety of salad garnishes, such as cucumber, carrots, beets, celery, pineapple, cantaloupe, or honeydew melon. Just before serving, sprinkle the salad with the crispy, deep-fried cracklings of duck skin for an interesting textural contrast.

1 4- or 5-pound Roast Duckling (page 130), skinned, boned, and cubed (4 to 5 cups)

Marinade

⅓ cup Commander's Dressing (page 52)
⅔ cup Commander's French Dressing (page 53)
¼ to ½ cup honey, to taste

---

6 cups mixed salad greens
1 can (15 ounces) hearts of palm, drained and sliced
½ cup thinly cut green beans or haricots verts, blanched until just tender
2 tablespoons Commander's Dressing

Garnish

½ cup walnut halves
1 pint fresh raspberries and/or blueberries
12 slices cucumber
12 broccoli flowerets, blanched
6 lemon wedges
6 half slices fresh pineapple
12 small wedges cantaloupe
12 small wedges honeydew melon
12 strawberries
6 stalks hearts of celery
6 carrot sticks
6 parsley sprigs
6 tablespoons crumbled cooked bacon
6 tablespoons crumbled blue cheese
24 julienne strips raw beets

1 Cut duck skin into julienne strips and set aside.

2 Mix together marinade ingredients and marinate the duck meat for twenty-four hours.

3 Just before serving, deep-fry the duck skin until crispy in oil heated to 350°. Drain on paper towel.

4 *To serve:* Toss salad greens with hearts of palm, green beans, and 2 tablespoons Commander's dressing. Divide onto 6 large chilled salad plates, keeping the greens a little to one side of the plate. Top with marinated duck.

5 Garnish the duck with the crisp duck skin, walnut halves, and berries. Opposite each serving arrange 2 slices cucumber, 2 broccoli flowerets, 1 lemon wedge, ½ slice pineapple, 2 wedges each cantaloupe and honeydew melon, 2 strawberries, 1 celery stalk, 1 carrot stick, a cluster of parsley, 1 tablespoon each crumbled bacon and cheese, and 4 strips beets.

Note: Oriental garnish books are excellent references for attractive and unusual methods of garnishing.

California Salad

SERVES 8 AS SIDE DISH

A simple and sunny salad inspired by California, this dish combines fruits, nuts, and raisins with a honey-yogurt dressing. For variety you can add fresh seasonal fruits such as strawberries or melon. You can also use different kinds of nuts—peanuts or slivered almonds, for instance. Improvise with whatever strikes your fancy in the market, as long as it's fresh and beautiful.

Honey-Yogurt Dressing

(MAKES 2½ CUPS)

- 1 pint plain yogurt
- Juice of 2 lemons
- 3 tablespoons honey
- Salt and white pepper to taste

- 1 head Boston lettuce, torn into bite-size pieces
- 4 avocados, peeled, pit removed, and sliced
- 1 cup grapefruit sections
- ½ cup walnut halves
- ¼ cup seedless raisins

1 Put dressing ingredients in blender container and blend at low speed for 10 seconds.

2 Mix salad ingredients in salad bowl. Serve on salad plates with dressing on the side.

Chicken Salad with Fresh Fruit

SERVES 4 AS ENTREE

This is a beautiful and healthy way to use leftover chicken or turkey. The diced meat is mixed with celery, green onions, pineapple, apples, and raisins, tossed in mayonnaise spiked with Worcestershire sauce and garnished with beautiful ripe red strawberries, bananas, and toasted almonds. The contrasting colors, textures, and flavors are pleasing to the eye as well as the palate. Serve with a Riesling or a Gewürztraminer wine.

- 3 cups cooked diced chicken or turkey
- 1 cup finely chopped celery
- 1 cup minced green onions
- 1 cup finely chopped pineapple
- 1 cup finely chopped apple
- ¼ cup seedless raisins

Homemade Mayonnaise

(MAKES 1¼ CUPS)

- 1 egg
- Juice of ½ medium lemon or 2 tablespoons lemon juice or red wine vinegar
- ¼ teaspoon dry mustard
- ⅛ teaspoon salt
- 1 teaspoon Worcestershire sauce
- 1 cup salad oil (part olive oil is excellent), at room temperature

---

- 4 large lettuce leaves

Garnish

- Strawberries or other berries in season
- Bananas, peeled and quartered
- Toasted almonds

1 In mixing bowl combine chicken, celery, green onions, pineapple, apple, and raisins. Refrigerate while making the mayonnaise.

2 *To make mayonnaise:* Break the egg into container of an electric blender. Add lemon juice (or wine vinegar), mustard, salt, Worcestershire sauce, and ¼ cup of oil. Cover and blend at low speed. Remove cover and *immediately* pour in remaining oil in a steady stream. Do *not* add it drop by drop, or the blender will liquefy the egg and the mayonnaise will not thicken.

3 Combine chicken mixture with ½ cup of mayonnaise.

4 *To serve:* Line each salad plate with a lettuce leaf and top with about 1½ cups chicken salad. Top with 2 additional tablespoons mayonnaise and garnish with berries, bananas, and toasted almonds.

Note: Should the mayonnaise fail to thicken, pour it into a large measuring cup or jug. Break another egg into blender container. Add ¼ cup of the mayonnaise mixture and try again, adding the unthickened mayonnaise in place of the oil. Store any leftover mayonnaise in a covered jar in the refrigerator. It will keep for a couple of weeks.

Fried Chicken Salad

SERVES 4 AS ENTREE

One of our most popular new entree salads, this is an interesting combination of deep-fried diced chicken breasts on salad greens tossed with a special blend of Commander's dressing and honey, champagne, and Parmesan cheese, and garnished with fresh fruits and vegetables. Serve with warm French bread or our Commander's Garlic Bread *(see page 16)**.*

- Salt and freshly ground black pepper to taste
- Dash of granulated or powdered garlic
- ½ cup all-purpose flour
- 1 egg, lightly beaten
- ½ cup milk
- 4 chicken breasts, skinned, boned, and cubed
- Oil for deep-frying

Special Fried Chicken Salad Dressing

(MAKES 1 CUP)

- ¾ cup Commander's Dressing (page 52)
- 1 tablespoon grated Parmesan cheese
- 2 tablespoons honey
- 5 tablespoons champagne

- 4 cups mixed salad greens torn into bite-size pieces

Garnish

- Seasonal fruits and vegetables

1 Mix together salt and pepper, garlic, and flour. Beat together egg and milk. Dredge chicken cubes in seasoned flour, then dip in egg mixture, and dredge again in flour. Deep-fry chicken cubes until golden brown in oil or shortening heated to 350°. Drain on paper towel and cool to room temperature.

2 Mix together dressing ingredients.

3 *To serve:* Toss chicken cubes with 4 teaspoons of dressing and set aside. Toss salad greens with rest of dressing and pile on one side of salad plates. Put a quarter of the chicken cubes in the center of each serving of salad greens and garnish with fruits and vegetables.

Egg Dishes

Eggs are one of our family's favorite foods—for breakfast, brunch, a light dinner, or late supper after the theater. Not only nutritious and economical, they can be prepared in an infinite variety of ways—from simple omelets to elaborate poached egg dishes with grand sauces to elegant soufflés. Supposedly there was once a French gentleman and gourmet who loved eggs so much he had his chef prepare them every morning of his life and never had them the same way twice!

Eggs are an essential part of the traditional hearty New Orleans breakfast, which originated in the late nineteenth century. At that time, restaurants in the French Market (the most famous of which was Madame Begué's, opened in 1881) would cater to tradesmen, merchants, and butchers who had been awake and working since 4:00 A.M., by serving full, hearty meals midmorning. Word got around about these early-morning feasts, and a wonderful tradition was started.

Another reason breakfasts are so important here is that New Orleans has always been a predominantly Catholic community. When you went to Mass on Sunday, you went hungry. (You were allowed to revel and drink on Saturday but were not allowed to eat anything after midnight if you were going to take Communion.) Hot rice cakes, or "calas," used to be sold by black women outside the churches in town to stave off hunger, and then most families would retire to one of New Orleans' fine restaurants for a luxurious breakfast.

Were we following nineteenth-century style, a serious breakfast at Commander's might start with grilled grapefruit, then Creole cream cheese topped with fresh, sweet strawberries, followed by eggs Hussarde, eggs Basin Street, or eggs Commander, then trout with roasted pecans or veal grillades, and finally climax with

bananas Foster and a steamy café au lait or a liquor-laced café brûlot.

At Commander's we are constantly creating new egg dishes to put on our Jazz Brunch menu. Some of the most recent additions to our repertoire are eggs soubise, poached eggs on grilled sausage topped with a lovely light leek sauce; eggs Basin Street, poached eggs on rice fritters sauced with spicy red beans; and eggs Commander, Holland rusks covered with ham cream sauce, topped with poached eggs and béarnaise sauce and served with our special sausage patties.

All our egg dishes are based on poached eggs or omelets and are basically simple to prepare. What makes them unusual is the combination of ingredients and the luxurious sauces.

If you're entertaining, light German wines go well with eggs—for instance, a Bernkasteler with a spicy dish like eggs Basin Street. Followed by lots of strong, hot New Orleans café au lait, New Orleans' grand breakfasts are among our special pleasures.

Chapter opening illustration: *The Jazz Brunch at Commander's has lots of colored balloons and two strolling bands.*

Eggs Commander

SERVES 6

The Jazz Brunch at our restaurant is so popular that we are always looking for new combinations to add excitement to the menu. In eggs Commander, one of our newest creations, Holland rusks or English muffins are covered with a savory ham cream sauce, topped with poached eggs and béarnaise sauce, and served with our own homemade sausage patties.

Ham Cream Sauce

- 1 cup finely chopped or diced ham
- 2 tablespoons chopped onions
- 2 cups Béchamel Sauce (page 198), heated

Commander's Homemade Sausage

(MAKES 12 PATTIES)

- ½ pound finely ground beef
- ½ pound finely ground pork
- ½ pound finely ground veal
- 3 cloves of garlic, minced
- 2 teaspoons salt
- ¾ cup chopped green onion tops
- ½ teaspoon nutmeg
- ⅓ teaspoon thyme
- 1½ teaspoons freshly ground black pepper
- 2 teaspoons cumin powder
- ½ teaspoon cayenne pepper

- 12 Holland rusks or 6 toasted English muffins, split
- 12 poached eggs
- 2 cups Béarnaise Sauce (page 196)

Garnish

Sprigs of parsley

1 *To make the ham cream sauce:* Sauté ham and onion in a little of the ham fat (if the ham has no fat, use 1 tablespoon butter). Add to hot cream sauce and mix well. Set aside.

2 *To make the sausage patties:* Mix sausage ingredients together well. Roll into a cylinder approximately 1½ inches in diameter and roughly 1 foot long, using aluminum foil to roll and wrap it in. Seal tightly and freeze until mixture hardens (this will take approximately 1½ hours). Remove from freezer and cut into ½-inch-thick slices. Fry slices in large skillet over medium high heat until well browned on both sides. Drain on paper towel.

3 Put 2 Holland rusks or English muffin halves on each warmed plate. Ladle 2 to 4 tablespoons hot ham cream sauce over each. Put 1 poached egg on each. Spoon a dollop of béarnaise sauce on each egg and put 2 sausage patties beside the rusks. Garnish with sprig of parsley.

Eggs Benedict

SERVES 6

The original classic French poached egg dish, eggs Benedict is suitable for any occasion, from the simplest to the most elegant. Two Holland rusks or English muffin halves are covered with slices of sautéed Canadian bacon, and each is topped with a poached egg and creamy hollandaise sauce and garnished with a slice of truffle. If you are making this for a large group, the eggs can be poached ahead of time, trimmed, and kept moist in a shallow pan of cool water. Reheat by slipping each egg into boiling water for a minute just before serving.

- 12 thin slices Canadian back bacon
- 12 Holland rusks or toasted English muffins
- 12 soft-poached eggs
- 1½ cups Hollandaise Sauce (page 199)
- 12 thin slices black truffle

1 Broil or sauté bacon on both sides until lightly browned, about 5 minutes.

2 Put 2 Holland rusks or English muffin halves on each warmed plate and top with a slice of bacon. Put egg on the bacon and cover with hollandaise. Top each egg with a slice of truffle. Serve immediately.

Note: Toasted bread rounds called Holland rusks are available from gourmet food shops as well as some supermarkets.

Eggs Basin Street

SERVES 4

Red beans and rice is a basic Creole dish. It is traditionally served on Mondays; some say that it makes economical use of the ham bone left from Sunday dinner; others say that the rice soaks up the alcohol consumed over the weekend!

We never put red beans and rice on the menu, because we felt it was such a home-style dish. But since it is such a divine combination, we decided to try it with eggs. Poached eggs are placed on rice fritters and sauced with creamy red beans, spiced with onion, garlic, andouille sausage, and Louisiana Red Hot Sauce.

Red Beans

(MAKES 2 CUPS COOKED)

- 2 pounds dried red beans or kidney beans
- ¾ pound andouille sausage, sliced
- ½ pound ham or pickled pork
- 1 medium onion, coarsely chopped
- 3 cloves of garlic, minced
- 3 or 4 drops Louisiana Red Hot Sauce to taste
- Salt to taste

Rice Fritters (Calas)

- 2 eggs, beaten
- 1 cup self-rising flour
- 1 cup milk
- 2 cups cold cooked rice
- Oil for frying

- 8 soft-poached eggs

1 ■ *To cook the beans:* Soak the beans overnight in plenty of water to cover. Next day drain and empty into a large stockpot or Dutch oven. Cover with fresh water to 2 inches above beans. In a frying pan sauté sausage and ham for a few minutes. Remove meat and sauté onion and garlic in oil left in pan. Add everything to pot with beans, bring to a boil, and cook over medium heat until beans are soft and creamy, about 2 hours. Add hot sauce and salt to taste and stir frequently during cooking. Add a little more water from time to time if needed.

2 ■ *To make fritters:* Combine eggs, flour, milk, and rice. Blend well to the consistency of pancake batter. Spoon 8 dollops of batter into hot skillet and fry in small quantity of oil until brown on both sides, turning only once. Set fritters aside and keep warm while eggs poach.

3 ■ Put poached eggs on rice fritters and serve 2 per person. Spoon cooked red beans over the eggs and serve immediately.

Eggs St. Charles

SERVES 6

This dish is named after one of our grand avenues in New Orleans.

When planning Breakfast at Brennan's we felt constrained to use only eggs as a breakfast food, but at Commander's Palace, because fish is so good and so popular in New Orleans, we decided to put fish on the brunch menu. If you can't get fresh trout, red snapper or striped bass fillets will do nicely.

- 6 trout fillets (6 ounces each)
- 1 cup all-purpose flour, seasoned with Creole Seafood Seasoning (page 190)
- 8 tablespoons (1 stick) unsalted butter
- 12 soft-poached eggs
- 1 cup Hollandaise Sauce (page 199)

1 Dredge trout fillets in seasoned flour and quickly sauté in butter over medium heat until lightly brown on both sides, turning only once.

2 For each serving, put a fillet of trout on a warmed plate. Top with 2 poached eggs and ladle hollandaise sauce over all.

Eggs Hussarde

SERVES 6

When creating the original Breakfast at Brennan's menu, we thought eggs Benedict too ordinary and added marchand de vins sauce and grilled tomato. The dish looks rich, but it tastes light. It has since become one of the most popular egg dishes in New Orleans.

- 3 tomatoes, halved
- 12 thin slices Canadian back bacon
- 12 Holland rusks or 6 toasted English muffins, split
- 1¾ cups Marchand de Vins Sauce (page 198)
- 12 soft poached eggs
- 1½ cups Hollandaise Sauce (page 199)

1 Broil or bake tomato halves until hot throughout, about 5 to 7 minutes.

2 Broil bacon on both sides. Set tomatoes and bacon aside and keep warm.

3 For each serving, put 2 Holland rusks or English muffin halves on a warmed plate. Cover with marchand de vins sauce. Put 1 slice bacon on each, top with a poached egg, and cover with hollandaise sauce. Put a tomato half beside each serving. Serve immediately.

Eggs Soubise

SERVES 4

Created by chef Gerhard Brill, eggs soubise is an elegant new dish combining sausage and poached eggs with a light leek and onion sauce. You can substitute any sausage you wish with slices 3½ to 4 inches in diameter and ½ inch thick.

- 8 slices sausage
- 2 tomatoes
- 2 tablespoons freshly grated Parmesan cheese

Soubise Sauce

(MAKES 2 CUPS)

- ½ cup coarsely chopped onions
- ½ cup thinly sliced white portion of leeks
- 2 tablespoons (¼ stick) unsalted butter
- ½ teaspoon freshly ground black pepper
- ½ teaspoon Creole Meat Seasoning (page 190)
- 2 tablespoons all-purpose flour
- 2 cups heavy cream
- Dash of salt

- 8 poached eggs

1 ■ Grill or broil sausage slices. Drain and keep warm.

2 ■ Cut ripe tomatoes in half crosswise and sprinkle the cut surface with Parmesan cheese. Grill until cheese and tomato are slightly bubbling. Set aside and keep warm.

3 ■ *To make the sauce:* Put the onions, leeks, and butter in a sauté pan. Cook over low heat until onions are transparent. Add black pepper and meat seasoning. Stir in flour and blend well. Add cream and continue to cook, stirring constantly, until mixture is the consistency of a medium cream sauce. Add a dash of salt to taste. If not using immediately, keep over hot water until ready to serve.

4 ■ Put 2 pieces of grilled sausage on each warmed plate. Put a poached egg on top of each slice of sausage. Put half a tomato on the side of the plate and top the eggs with the soubise sauce. Serve immediately.

Eggs Creole

SERVES 4

A soulful, spicy new dish, eggs Creole is a combination of grits, sausage, poached eggs, and Creole sauce. Practically a meal in itself, it could make a hearty winter luncheon entree, served with a salad, a slice of Brie, and your favorite white wine.

Fried Grits

(MAKES 8 ROUNDS)

Hominy grits (not instant)
2 tablespoons (¼ stick) unsalted butter
1 cup finely chopped andouille sausage or spicy sausage like kielbasa
4 tablespoons shredded Cheddar cheese
Dash of salt
All-purpose flour for dusting
1 egg beaten with 1 tablespoon milk
Seasoned bread crumbs
Oil or fat for deep-frying

Creole Sauce (page 197)

---

8 poached eggs
4 slices sausage, ½ inch thick, broiled

1 *To make grits:* A day in advance, prepare 4 servings of hominy grits according to directions on package. When cooked, remove from heat and stir in butter, sausage, cheese, and salt. Spoon into a baking pan to a depth of about ½ inch and chill for at least 24 hours. The next day, turn the grits out onto waxed paper and with a glass or biscuit cutter cut out rounds about 2½ inches in diameter. Dust the cutouts with flour, dip in egg and milk mixture, and coat with bread crumbs. Just before assembling eggs Creole, fry the rounds in deep fat heated to 400°. Drain on paper towels and keep hot.

2 Make Creole sauce if not made a day ahead.

3 Put 2 rounds of fried grits on each warmed plate. Top each round of grits with a poached egg and ladle Creole sauce over. Arrange one sausage slice on each plate. Serve immediately.

Eggs de la Salle

SERVES 6

This is a luxurious brunch dish you'll love: a base of deviled crab cakes topped with poached eggs and a sauce flavored with brandy and red wine, enriched with an assortment of fresh wild mushrooms. We frequently use chanterelles, morels, and enoki, but since the success of the sauce demands that the mushrooms be fresh, use whatever fresh wild mushrooms you can find.

The inspiration for the dish came from Leon Lianides's Coach House Restaurant in New York. Crab cakes rarely appear on the menus of first-class restaurants, but Leon serves them with great success, and now we have revived them too. We serve them as an appetizer with a reduction of Creole sauce or, as here, a base for eggs de la Salle.

Deviled Crab Cakes

(MAKES 12)

- ¼ cup chopped white onions
- ¼ cup chopped celery
- ¼ cup chopped green bell pepper
- 1 large clove of garlic, finely chopped
- Pinch of thyme
- ½ pound (2 sticks) unsalted butter
- 1 pound fresh lumb crab meat, shells carefully removed
- 2 tablespoons chopped green onions
- Pinch of cayenne pepper
- Dash of Worcestershire sauce
- ¼ cup grated Romano cheese
- 2 cups coarsely ground fresh bread crumbs
- 1 large egg, lightly beaten
- Salt and freshly ground black pepper to taste

Wild Mushroom Sauce

(MAKES 1½ CUPS)

- 4 medium shallots (2 ounces), chopped
- 4 ounces wild mushrooms (morels, chanterelles, etc.)
- ¼ cup (½ stick) unsalted butter
- 2 ounces cultivated American mushrooms
- 1 ounce brandy
- ¼ cup dry red wine
- ¾ cup Demi-glace (page 193)
- ¼ cup heavy cream
- Salt and freshly ground black pepper to taste

- 12 soft-poached eggs

1 ■ *To make the crab cakes:* Sauté onions, celery, green bell pepper, garlic, and thyme in half the butter until onion is transparent. Add crab meat, green onions, cayenne pepper, and Worcestershire sauce. Simmer for 10 minutes, occasionally tossing very gently.

2 Remove from heat and gently mix in cheese, bread crumbs, egg, and salt and pepper. Pat gently into 12 round cakes ½ inch thick and sauté in remaining butter until golden on both sides, turning only once. Keep warm until ready to serve.

3 *To make the sauce:* Sauté shallots and all mushrooms in butter in a skillet, stirring constantly, for 1 minute. Add brandy, wine, demi-glace, and cream. Correct seasoning with salt and pepper if needed and simmer for about 5 minutes.

4 *To serve:* Put 2 poached eggs on top of 2 crab cakes and ladle over a good spoonful of sauce.

Eggs Cordon Bleu

SERVES 6

This is the classic cordon bleu combination of ham and cheese, "Creolized" with a lavish marchand de vins sauce. The quality of the ham and cheese is very important. You may use any kind of ham you like; Black Forest ham is especially delicious.

- 6 slices Swiss cheese, 1 ounce each
- 6 slices ham, 8 inches by 4 inches
- Flour for dredging
- Egg wash (1 lightly beaten egg combined with 1 cup milk)
- 1 cup dry bread crumbs
- 8 tablespoons (1 stick) unsalted butter
- 12 soft-poached eggs
- 1¾ cups Marchand de Vins Sauce (page 198)

1 Fold each slice of cheese in half. Fold a slice of ham around each slice of cheese. Dredge ham and cheese in flour, dip in egg wash, then coat well with bread crumbs.

2 Melt butter over moderate heat in a large skillet and sauté breaded ham-cheese until golden brown on all sides.

3 Put 1 slice of the sautéed ham-cheese on each warmed plate. Top with 2 poached eggs and cover generously with marchand de vins sauce. Serve immediately.

Eggs Elizabeth

SERVES 4

Named after Betty Hoffman, who worked at Commander's for years on special projects (we call her our own James Beard), eggs Elizabeth is a marvelous juxtaposition of colors and textures. Grilled Canadian bacon, deep-fried eggplant, and poached eggs are topped with a spicy Creole version of the classic sauce choron.

New Orleans has a large Italian population and we all love eggplant here. To deep-fat fry eggplant, it is important that the oil (shortening is best) be very hot (350°) so that the vegetable needs to cook only 2 or 3 minutes. This way it will not absorb the oil. Or, if you prefer even less oil, the eggplant may be sautéed slowly.

- 1 medium eggplant
- 1 egg, lightly beaten
- Seasoned bread crumbs
- Shortening or oil for frying
- 8 slices Canadian back bacon
- 8 poached eggs
- 2 cups Choron Sauce (page 197)

1 ■ Peel eggplant deeply and slice into 8 rounds ¼ inch thick. Dip slices in beaten egg, then in crumbs, and fry until golden brown in shortening or oil heated to 350°. Drain on paper towels and keep warm until ready to serve.

2 ■ Grill or broil bacon and put 2 slices on each warmed plate. Top with 2 slices fried eggplant. Put a poached egg on each and ladle sauce over eggs.

Eggs Sardou

SERVES 4

The first of New Orlean's elaborate, elegant egg dishes, eggs Sardou was created in 1908 at Antoine's on the occasion of a dinner he hosted for the French playwright Victorien Sardou. A timeless classic, it combines creamed spinach, artichoke bottoms, poached eggs, and hollandaise sauce. Preparing fresh artichoke bottoms takes time and should be done in advance. They can be reheated in a little hot water. If you are pressed for time, use canned.

For a delicious variation, substitute fresh lump crab meat, lightly sautéed, for the eggs.

Creamed Spinach

- 2 pounds fresh spinach
- 2 cups water
- 1½ tablespoons unsalted butter
- ¼ cup finely chopped green onions
- 1 cup Béchamel Sauce (page 198)
- ½ teaspoon salt
- ¼ teaspoon freshly ground black pepper

- 8 cooked artichoke bottoms, fresh or canned
- 8 poached eggs
- 2 cups Hollandaise Sauce (page 199)

1 *To make creamed spinach:* Wash spinach thoroughly and discard thick heavy stems. Bring water to a rapid boil, add spinach, and cook until wilted and barely tender. Add ice or ice water to stop the cooking and let drain for 10 minutes. Spinach should be very dry.

2 Melt butter in a large skillet. Add green onions and sauté, stirring, for 2 minutes. Add spinach and sauté for 2 minutes longer. Stir in béchamel sauce and salt and pepper. Set aside and keep warm.

3 *To serve:* Put a quarter of the creamed spinach on each warmed plate and top with 2 warm artichoke bottoms. Put 2 poached eggs on the artichoke bottoms and ladle over ½ cup hollandaise sauce. Serve immediately.

Four-Egg Omelet

SERVES 1

Easy and elegant, rich and refined, a folded omelet filled and topped with fresh New Orleans seafood or spicy Creole Sauce (page 197) is always a satisfying lunch, served with a fresh green salad and white wine. An almost unlimited variety of fillings can be used; for instance, we use sautéed crawfish in season. A main luncheon omelet at Commander's uses 4 eggs.

- 4 eggs
- 1 tablespoon butter
- Sauce and filling (see individual omelet recipes)

1 ■ Beat eggs lightly. Do not overbeat or they will become thin.

2 ■ Heat butter in an omelet pan, and just as it is beginning to give off a nutty aroma (but not to brown), pour in the eggs. Cook over moderate heat until almost set. Do not overcook. The omelet should be moist.

3 ■ When it is almost finished, put a spoonful of sauce and filling on it, fold, and turn out on a warmed plate. Top with more sauce and serve immediately.

Creamed Oyster Omelet

(SAUCE AND FILLING FOR FOUR 4-EGG OMELETS)

- 4 teaspoons butter
- 4 teaspoons flour
- 24 oysters, oyster liquor reserved
- 2 cups heavy cream
- 8 green onions, minced
- 1 bay leaf
- 2 teaspoons Creole Seafood Seasoning (page 190)

1 ■ Melt butter in a small sauté pan, stir in flour, and cook, stirring, just until roux bubbles and turns a light amber in color.

2 ■ In a pan combine oysters and their liquor and cream. Add green onions, bay leaf, and seafood seasoning. Bring to a simmer and poach oysters just until edges begin to curl. Add the roux and simmer, stirring gently, for about 1 minute. Set aside until ready to make omelets.

3 ■ When each omelet is almost cooked, put 3 oysters and some of the sauce inside. Fold, turn out on a warmed plate, and top with another 3 oysters and more sauce.

Crab Meat Omelet

(SAUCE AND FILLING FOR FOUR 4-EGG OMELETS)

8 green onions, minced
4 teaspoons Creole Seafood Seasoning (page 190)
4 tablespoons (½ stick) unsalted butter
6 ounces lump crab meat, shells carefully removed
1 cup Hollandaise Sauce (page 199)

1 ■ Sauté green onions and seafood seasoning in butter for 2 minutes, stirring constantly. Add crab meat and mix gently; do not stir.

2 ■ Add 4 tablespoons hollandaise sauce to the mixture when ready to make the omelets.

3 ■ Make omelets and top each with remaining hollandaise sauce.

Seafood

New Orleans is blessed with a super-abundance of fresh local seafood—both fish and shellfish—in unsurpassed variety. A haven for fishermen for hundreds of years, New Orleans has naturally developed a cuisine that specializes in seafood, prepared in ways that traditionally have been a marriage of the French, Spanish, and African influences.

From the waters of the Gulf of Mexico come such famous saltwater varieties as pompano, our most renowned gourmet eating fish; redfish and red snapper, with their distinctive flavors, the basis of many Creole dishes; our native flounder, which many find superior in flavor to the imported French and English soles; speckled trout, a favorite in New Orleans cuisine, especially for breakfast; and Spanish mackerel. Among freshwater fish, the most frequently used are bass, catfish, and brook trout.

As for shellfish, we are daily seduced by such specialties as local oysters, ubiquitous in New Orleans and prized by epicures for their superior flavor and quality, which are prepared by Creole cooks in more different ways than in any other cuisine; large lake shrimp; smaller, delicate river shrimp; crayfish or crawfish, a world-renowned delicacy that we have in great quantity; crabs—hard-shell crabs, buster crabs, and soft-shell crabs; and green turtle. The variety and abundance of seafood in New Orleans combine to make a bouillabaisse said to rival that of Marseille.

Some of the classic Creole seafood preparations developed over the centuries have included pompano en papillotte, trout almondine, oysters Rockefeller, shrimp Creole, crab meat ravigote or rémoulade, and crawfish etoufée. We have been working for the last five years to adapt these and other dishes to lighter contemporary tastes. For example, one of the most popular fish dishes on our current menu is grilled or "blackened" redfish, which came about when we asked chef Gerhard Brill, who is a fisherman, to "prepare a fish the way you would if you had just caught it and were cooking it right there on the side of the river." He said he would season it highly with lots of our special Creole spices, and cook it in a very hot pan over a blazing fire for mere minutes, searing it almost black on the outside to retain the flavor and moistness. Another new item, trout with roasted pecans, bathed in pecan butter, makes use of our local fresh pecans, instead of the almonds we used to get from California.

Pompano en papillotte, or pompano steamed in a paper bag, is an old classic French recipe in which the fish is heavily sauced. For a while we simply took it off the menu; then, at the suggestion of Ella's son, Alex Brennan, we started steaming the pompano in its own juices, serving a light hollandaise on the side. It became a much lighter dish and is now one of the most popular items on the menu and a good example of what we mean by the new Haute Creole.

Instead of oysters Rockefeller or oysters Bienville, we do a simpler, lighter oysters à la marinière. In place of a crawfish etoufée, we make a crawfish sauté with fresh vegetables. We have even lightened our shrimp creole, replacing the base of tomato paste with a well-seasoned light tomato purée.

We have also broadened the menu at Commander's to encompass Oriental-inspired dishes such as shrimp with stir-fried vegetables, and coconut and beer-battered shrimp with sweet and sour sauce. We have even put several pasta dishes on our menu, such as shrimp and fettuccine. Though many people think of New Orleans as rice country, we think pasta is a nice change.

Chapter opening illustration: *In the Louisiana bayous, fishermen catch fresh crawfish for many wonderful Creole dishes.*

Shrimp and Fettuccine

SERVES 4

Recently, when pasta became so popular, we put it on the menu at another of our restaurants, Mr. B's in the French Quarter, where it met with such success that we adopted it at Commander's. Although pasta was never part of Creole cuisine, it is very much a part of New Orleans because of the large Italian population here. Use only fresh shrimp, fresh pasta, and the lushest red tomatoes you can find.

We also serve pasta with crawfish tails. Substitute spinach noodles for fettuccine for a beautiful color combination.

- 8 tablespoons (1 stick) unsalted butter
- 2 cloves of garlic, minced
- 4 teaspoons minced parsley
- ½ onion, diced
- 4 fresh mushrooms, sliced
- 4 tablespoons peeled, seeded, and chopped fresh tomato
- ½ cup chopped green onions
- 2 teaspoons Creole Seafood Seasoning (page 190)
- ¼ cup Shrimp Stock (page 191)
- 2 cups cooked fettuccine noodles (12 ounces dry pasta)
- 24 medium shrimp, peeled and deveined
- ½ cup dry white wine

1 ■ Melt half the butter in a large saucepan and sauté the garlic, parsley, onions, mushrooms, tomato, green onions, and seafood seasoning for 30 seconds, stirring gently. Add stock and simmer until onions are transparent.

2 ■ Add the cooked fettuccine, the shrimp, and the wine and simmer until liquid is almost evaporated.

3 ■ Remove pan from heat, add remaining butter, and stir gently until butter is melted and sauce is creamy. Serve immediately.

Shrimp Victoria

SERVES 6

This is a classic New Orleans shrimp dish in a very rich cream sauce thickened with sour cream and flavored with onions, green onions, and sweet basil. We serve it over steamed fluffy white rice or, alternatively, tossed with pasta shells.

- 3 tablespoons butter
- 3 tablespoons flour
- 3 cups Shrimp or Seafood Stock (page 191)
- 3 tablespoons sour cream
- ⅓ pound fresh mushrooms, sliced
- ¼ cup minced white onions
- 4 green onion tops, minced
- 2 tablespoons chopped sweet basil
- ¼ cup heavy cream
- 60 medium shrimp (approximately 2 pounds), peeled and deveined
- Salt and freshly ground black pepper to taste

1 ■ Melt butter in a small saucepan, add flour, and whisk over moderate heat until roux is smooth, bubbling, and pale blond. Set asidc.

2 ■ Put stock in a 3-quart saucepan and bring to a rolling boil. Add the roux and mix well. Add sour cream and blend thoroughly. Add mushrooms, onions, green onions, and basil and simmer for 5 minutes. Add cream and stir well.

3 ■ Continue to simmer on low heat and add shrimp. Correct seasoning with salt and pepper if needed and simmer for 5 minutes.

Coconut Beer Shrimp with Sweet and Tangy Dipping Sauce

SERVES 6

Of Caribbean and Oriental inspiration, coconut beer shrimp was put on the menu at the request of a good local customer, whose favorite dish it was. We "Creolized" it by adding Creole seafood seasoning to the batter and Creole mustard to the sweet and sour sauce. It's a marvelous hors d'oeuvre for a party. Leave the tails on the shrimp so they can be picked up with the fingers.

4 eggs
1 cup beer
3½ teaspoons Creole Seafood Seasoning (page 190)
1¼ cups all-purpose flour
2 tablespoons baking powder
48 large raw shrimp, peeled but with tails on, deveined
1½ to 2 cups shredded coconut, fresh or moist-pack
Vegetable oil for deep-frying

Sweet and Tangy Dipping Sauce

2 cups orange marmalade
¼ cup Creole mustard or Dijon mustard
3 tablespoons shredded horseradish

1 ■ Combine eggs, beer, 1 teaspoon seafood seasoning, flour, and baking powder. Blend well.

2 ■ Season shrimp with remaining seafood seasoning.

3 ■ Dip the shrimp in beer batter and roll in coconut. Fry in oil heated to 350° in a deep-fat fryer, wok, or deep saucepan. The oil should be at least 1½ inches deep. Drop shrimp in a few at a time and fry until golden brown. Remove and drain on paper towel.

4 ■ Blend together dipping sauce ingredients.

5 ■ *To serve:* Put a small bowl of the sweet and tangy sauce in the center of each plate. Arrange 8 shrimp around it and serve immediately.

Shrimp Croustade

SERVES 6

A simple and elegant appetizer for a dinner party, shrimp croustade is a flaky puff pastry shell filled with sautéed shrimp in a sauce of heavily reduced shrimp stock, Creole seafood seasoning, fresh dill, tarragon, basil, white wine, and cream. Use a pastry shell about 3 inches in diameter; for an appetizer fill it only halfway; for an entree fill it to the top. Puff pastry is tricky to make, and unless you are experienced, it is easier to buy the pastry shells already made. Serve this with a well-chilled Chablis or dry California Chardonnay.

- 72 medium shrimp (about 2 pounds), peeled and deveined
- 2 teaspoons Creole Seafood Seasoning (page 190)
- 3/4 cup (1 1/2 sticks) unsalted butter
- 1/4 cup minced shallots
- 1/2 cup dry white wine
- 3 cups heavily reduced Shrimp or Fish Stock (page 191)
- 1 cup heavy cream
- 6 frozen puff pastry shells, baked

1 Season shrimp with Creole seafood seasoning.

2 Heat half the butter in a heavy iron skillet. Add shallots and sauté until transparent. Add shrimp and cook for 2 minutes. Remove shrimp and keep warm.

3 Add wine to pan and cook, stirring, for 1 minute. Add stock and cook until reduced to half, about 30 minutes. Add cream and continue to cook until sauce is reduced by half. Add remaining butter and swirl pan above the heat until butter is melted and sauce is glazed. Add shrimp to sauce and simmer for 2 minutes longer.

4 Serve in patty shells.

Shrimp Creole

SERVES 6 TO 8

Another classic New Orleans dish, shrimp Creole was just put back on our menu in a new light Haute Creole version. It used to be made with thick tomato paste, but now we use only fresh diced tomatoes. The result is not a heavy sauce, but rather a beautiful glaze. A good party dish when you don't know exactly how many guests to expect, shrimp Creole is often served with seafood jambalaya (rice cooked down in a Creole sauce with seafood and sausage), as the dry and wet textures complement each other.

- 6 tablespoons (¾ stick) unsalted butter
- 1 cup fine julienne-cut onions
- 1 cup fine julienne-cut green bell pepper
- 2 stalks celery, cut into fine julienne strips
- 2 cloves of garlic, thinly sliced
- 1 bay leaf
- 2 tablespoons paprika
- 2 cups diced fresh tomatoes
- 1 cup tomato juice
- 4 teaspoons Worcestershire sauce
- 4 teaspoons Louisiana Red Hot Sauce
- 1½ tablespoons cornstarch
- ½ cup water
- 3 pounds shrimp, peeled and deveined

1 ■ Melt 2 tablespoons butter in a sauté pan and sauté onion, green bell pepper, celery, garlic, and bay leaf for a minute or two. Before the onion becomes transparent, add paprika (for color), tomatoes, and tomato juice. Stir well. Add Worcestershire sauce and red hot sauce and simmer until volume is reduced by a fourth and the vegetables are soft.

2 ■ Mix cornstarch and water and stir into the sauce. Cook, stirring, for about 2 minutes to cook the cornstarch.

3 ■ Sauté the shrimp in the remaining butter until pink and tender, about 5 minutes, stirring constantly. Pour sauce over shrimp and toss to coat well. Serve with fluffy cooked rice.

Crawfish and Pasta with Stir-Fried Vegetables

SERVES 6

A popular new cross-cultural dish that blends Italian pasta shells and zucchini, Louisiana crawfish and Creole seasonings, with Chinese cooking techniques. If you don't have crawfish stock, you can use fish stock. And if you can't get fresh crawfish tails, you can use fresh shrimp instead. We use pasta shells, but you could certainly substitute any other pasta with eye appeal. Remember, the spirit of the new Haute Creole cuisine is experimentation.

- 1 cup dried shell pasta
- 8 tablespoons (1 stick) unsalted butter
- 4 small onions, coarsely chopped
- 12 fresh mushrooms, quartered
- 4 small fresh tomatoes, peeled, seeded, and coarsely chopped
- 1 pound cooked crawfish tails, peeled and deveined, or cooked shrimp
- 2 teaspoons Creole Seafood Seasoning (page 190)
- 4 cloves of garlic, minced
- 1½ cups fine julienne-cut carrots
- 1½ cups fine julienne-cut celery
- 1½ cups fine julienne-cut turnips
- 1½ cups fine julienne-cut zucchini
- 1½ cups shredded cabbage
- Salt and freshly ground black pepper
- ½ cup Crawfish or Fish Stock (page 191)

Garnish

- 12 whole boiled crawfish or shrimp

1 Cook pasta according to package directions, *al dente*. Keep warm.

2 Melt butter in a sauté pan, add onions, mushrooms, and tomatoes, and sauté until onions are transparent. Add crawfish or shrimp, seafood seasoning, garlic, carrots, celery, turnips, zucchini, and cabbage. Stir gently. Simmer 1 minute. Add salt and pepper to taste and the stock. Cook until liquid is reduced by a third.

3 Serve over the pasta. Garnish each serving with 2 whole crawfish.

Sauté of Fresh Louisiana Crawfish

SERVES 4

This sauté of fresh Louisiana crawfish is a simple but spectacular dish—ideal for elegant entertaining. It is quick to assemble—all the ingredients can be organized ahead—and the final preparation takes a mere 2 minutes.

Make sure not to overcook the crawfish; they are more delicate than shrimp, so you must be more careful.

Crawfish Rice

- 4 tablespoons (½ stick) unsalted butter
- 1 medium onion, finely chopped
- 2 stalks celery, finely chopped
- 1 green bell pepper, finely chopped
- ½ pound cooked crawfish tails, peeled, deveined, and chopped*
- 1 cup raw rice
- 1⅔ cups Crawfish or Fish Stock (page 191), heated
- 1 teaspoon salt, or to taste

- 10 ounces (2 sticks plus 2 tablespoons) unsalted butter, softened
- 1 pound cooked crawfish tails, peeled and deveined*
- 1 cup chopped green onions
- 1 tablespoon Creole Seafood Seasoning (page 190)
- 1 tablespoon Worcestershire sauce

1 *To make the rice:* Melt butter in a saucepan over low heat. Add onion, celery, green bell pepper, and crawfish and sauté for 2 minutes. Add rice and mix well to coat rice with butter. Add boiling stock, bring liquid back to a boil, cover pot tightly, and simmer until rice is tender and all the liquid has been absorbed, about 20 minutes. Set aside and keep warm.

2 In a frying pan melt 2 tablespoons butter and sauté crawfish tails and green onions with seafood seasoning and Worcestershire sauce until hot, stirring constantly. Remove from heat. Add the remaining softened butter, a piece at a time, tossing mixture gently until butter is incorporated in the sauce and sauce is creamy.

3 Serve immediately with crawfish rice and French bread.

---

* One pound live crawfish yields ½ pound peeled cooked tails.

Trout in Leek Sauce

SERVES 2

One of our most popular new Haute Creole creations, trout in leek sauce is very light and delicate, inspired by French nouvelle cuisine, which popularized the leek. Actually, leeks have been used with seafood in Europe for hundreds of years. We use Gulf trout or speckled trout, cutting the fillet into 2-ounce pieces and arranging them in a decorative star shape. Champagne may be substituted for white wine to lighten the sauce. Garnished with fluted mushrooms or a fleuron of puff pastry, this is now one of the best new dishes on our menu.

- 8 tablespoons (1 stick) unsalted butter
- 1 cup fine julienne-cut white part of leeks
- 1 cup fine julienne-cut onions
- 6 thin strips peeled fresh tomato
- 1 teaspoon Creole Seafood Seasoning (page 190)
- 6 trout fillets, about 2 ounces each
- ½ cup dry white wine
- ½ cup heavily reduced Fish Stock (page 191)
- 6 fresh whole mushroom caps
- ½ cup heavy cream

1 Melt butter in sauté pan large enough to hold the 6 fillets without crowding. Scatter the leeks, onions, and tomato over bottom of sauté pan and sprinkle with seafood seasoning. Arrange fillets gently on this bed of vegetables. Add the wine, stock, and mushrooms. Bring to a boil, cover pan, and cook over low heat until fillets are done, about 5 minutes. Do not overcook.

2 Remove fish to a warm platter and put a mushroom on each fillet. Cook broth over high heat until it is reduced to ¼ cup. Add cream and stir gently. Simmer for 5 minutes, stirring constantly, then continue to cook until most of the liquid has evaporated.

3 Spoon the vegetable sauce over the fish and mushrooms and serve immediately.

Trout with Roasted Pecans and Creole Meunière Sauce

SERVES 6

This trout with two sauces is a simple, light, and unusual new dish. Trout almondine is classic Creole, but since New Orleans is, after all, pecan country, we decided to use local pecans. Trout fillets are lightly floured and quickly sautéed until golden brown, then gently covered with pecan butter, chopped roasted pecans, and piquant Creole meunière sauce. The pairing of pecan butter and chopped roasted pecans doubles the nutty flavor, and the crunchy texture of the nuts is a nice counterpoint to the smooth sauce. Serve with fresh vegetables like carrots for color, braised celery, or turnips.

- 1 cup shelled pecans
- 4 tablespoons (½ stick) unsalted butter, softened
- Juice of ½ medium lemon
- 1 teaspoon Worcestershire sauce

Creole Meunière Sauce

- 2 tablespoons cooking oil
- 2 tablespoons all-purpose flour
- 1½ cups Fish Stock (page 191)
- Salt and freshly ground black pepper to taste
- 8 tablespoons (1 stick) unsalted butter, cut into chunks and softened
- 2 tablespoons Worcestershire sauce
- Juice of 1 lemon
- ¼ cup chopped parsley

- 2 medium eggs, lightly beaten
- 1 cup milk
- 2 teaspoons Creole Seafood Seasoning (page 190)
- 1 cup all-purpose flour
- 6 trout fillets, 6 ounces each
- ½ cup Clarified Butter (page 195) or half cooking oil and half margarine

Garnish

- ½ cup reserved chopped roasted pecans
- Parsley sprigs
- Lemon wedges

1 Spread pecans on a cookie sheet and bake in a preheated 350° oven for 10 minutes. Coarsely chop half the roasted pecans and set aside for garnish. Put remaining half into container of a blender or food processor. Add butter, lemon juice, and Worcestershire sauce and blend to a smooth butter. Set aside.

2 *To make sauce:* Heat oil in a heavy skillet. Remove from heat and add flour. Return to heat and cook, stirring, until the roux becomes medium brown in color. Slowly whisk in stock, bring to a boil, stirring constantly, and simmer for 45 minutes. Correct seasoning. There should be about 1 cup sauce.

3 Transfer the brown fish sauce to a 2-quart saucepan and bring back to a quick simmer. Whisk in softened butter and Worcestershire sauce and continue to whisk until butter is absorbed. Add lemon juice and parsley. Whisk again briefly and remove from heat. This sauce should be used within 45 minutes of the time it is completed.

4 Combine eggs and milk, beating until well blended. Set aside.

5 Combine seafood seasoning and flour on waxed paper or in an aluminum pie plate. Dredge fillets in the seasoned flour to coat them well on both sides, dip in egg-milk mixture, then again in the seasoned flour.

6 Melt clarified butter in a large skillet over medium-high heat. Lay fillets carefully in the pan and sauté quickly, turning only once, until crisp and golden brown on both sides, about 2 minutes per side. Remove to a warm serving platter.

7 *To serve:* Put a filet on each plate and top with a heaping tablespoon of pecan butter, coating the entire fillet. Sprinkle with a heaping tablespoon of chopped roasted pecans. Cover trout and toppings with Creole meunière sauce and garnish with parsley and lemon wedges.

Crab Meat Lausanne

SERVES 4

This simple crab meat dish is bathed in Commander's special Creole meunière sauce, a distinctive variation on the classic butter sauce. Serve on top of buttered rice mixed with roasted slivered almonds.

- ½ pound (2 sticks) unsalted butter
- Juice of 2 lemons
- 4 teaspoons Worcestershire sauce
- 4 teaspoons Creole Meunière Sauce (page 194)
- 2 pounds lump crab meat, shells carefully removed
- 2 teaspoons Creole Seafood Seasoning (page 190)

1 Heat butter in sauté pan. Add lemon juice, Worcestershire sauce and Creole meunière sauce and whisk until well blended. Add crab meat and seafood seasoning. Stir gently over medium heat, being careful not to break the crab meat lumps.

2 When well mixed and thoroughly warm, serve over almond rice.

Crab Meat Imperial

SERVES 6

For those who love crab meat, the imperial version adds a piquant homemade Creole mayonnaise sauce. We serve it in coquille shells or ramekins, but it is a very versatile mixture and can be used as either a main course or an appetizer, or to stuff tomatoes, artichoke bottoms, or soft-shell crabs. Serve very hot.

- 1½ pounds lump crab meat, shells carefully removed
- 1 small green bell pepper, very finely chopped
- 1 pimiento, very finely chopped
- 2 green onions, finely chopped
- 2 egg yolks
- 1 tablespoon Worcestershire sauce
- Dash of Tabasco sauce
- 3 tablespoons plus 12 tablespoons Homemade Mayonnaise (page 66)
- 1 tablespoon Creole or Dijon mustard
- Salt and white pepper to taste

1 ■ Preheat oven to 350°.

2 ■ Combine crab meat with the chopped vegetables, egg yolks, Worcestershire sauce, Tabasco sauce, 3 tablespoons mayonnaise, mustard, and salt and pepper. Mix gently, being careful not to break up crab meat lumps.

3 ■ Spoon mixture into coquille shells or individual ramekins and top each with 2 tablespoons additional mayonnaise.

4 ■ Bake until tops are nicely browned, about 12 minutes.

Soft-Shell Crab Choron

SERVES 8

You should serve soft-shell crabs only when they are fresh and in season, usually from the beginning of April through August, depending on the weather. We serve them with Commander's version of a classic French choron sauce: Instead of blending béarnaise with tomato, we use Creole sauce.

Use shortening, not oil (it burns and is fatty), to fry the crabs, and take care not to overfry them—remove them with tongs after 3 minutes at 350°. At this temperature they do not become fatty because they don't have time to absorb the grease.

Choron Sauce

- 1 cup Creole Sauce (page 197)
- 1¼ cups Béarnaise Sauce (page 196)

- 8 large soft-shell crabs
- 16 medium shrimp, peeled and deveined
- ½ recipe of Crab Meat Imperial (page 98)
- 2 teaspoons Creole Seafood Seasoning (page 190)
- 1 cup all-purpose flour
- 1 egg, lightly beaten
- 1 cup milk
- Bread crumbs seasoned with Creole seafood seasoning
- Oil for deep-frying

1 *To make choron sauce:* Reduce 1 cup Creole sauce to ⅓ cup. Add the béarnaise sauce and mix well. It will keep at room temperature for 3 or 4 hours.

2 *To stuff the crabs:* Lift each shoulder and remove gills. Put a shrimp in each pocket where gills had been. Remove the soft top of the crab and fill with crab meat imperial stuffing.

3 Season the crabs with seafood seasoning and dust with flour. Combine egg and milk. Dip crab into egg mixture and then bread crumbs.

4 Deep-fry crabs in shortening heated to 350°: Hold the crab by body with tongs and fry the legs first, for about 30 seconds. This will cause the legs to fold up to the body. Then turn the crab upside down and place carefully in the hot shortening. Fry until golden brown, about 3 minutes.

5 Remove and drain on paper towel. Serve immediately with choron sauce.

Pompano en Papillotte

SERVES 4

This is an old New Orleans dish we have updated to the new lighter Haute Creole style. The pompano fillet is poached in its own juices in a parchment bag with oysters, shrimp, and mushrooms. We have lightened the sauce by taking the flour out and now serve the sauce on the side. The bag must be folded tightly so it fluffs up with air, and the pan must be oiled so the bag does not stick. When serving this for guests, cut open the parchment with a knife at the table and quickly roll back the paper with a fork for a dramatic presentation.

- 4 20-inch squares parchment paper*
- unsalted butter
- 8 pompano fillets from 4 1-pound pompano (save bones for stock)
- 8 freshly shucked oysters, drained
- 8 medium shrimp, peeled and deveined
- 4 large mushrooms, halved and blanched
- 1 teaspoon Creole Seafood Seasoning (page 190)

Papillotte Sauce

- 24 shrimp, peeled and deveined
- 24 oysters
- 2 tablespoons Creole Seafood Seasoning (page 190)
- 1 clove of garlic, minced
- ½ medium onion, minced
- 6 tablespoons (¾ stick) unsalted butter
- 4 cups Fish Stock (page 191), preferably made from pompano bones
- 2 cups heavy cream
- 1 cup champagne

1 ■ Preheat oven to 350°.

2 ■ Fold the parchment squares in half and cut into a large heart pattern. Open flat and butter the inside surface. On one inside half of each parchment heart put 2 fillets. On top of each fillet put 2 oysters, 2 shrimp, and a mushroom half. Sprinkle each serving with ¼ teaspoon seafood seasoning.

3 ■ Cover the fish with the other half of the parchment heart, matching the curved top and point at opposite end. Fold over the parchment where the two edges meet, starting at the wide top and working to the tip and sealing the paper in short overlapping folds. Put the sealed packages on an oiled baking sheet and bake for about 15 minutes.

4 ■ *To make the sauce:* Sprinkle shrimp and oysters with seafood seasoning and sauté with garlic and onion in 4 tablespoons butter until edges of oysters begin to curl.

---

* Parchment paper can be found in kitchen supply and gourmet shops.

5 ■ Add stock and bring to a boil, stirring. Remove oysters and shrimp and keep hot. Simmer stock until reduced by a third. Add cream and continue to cook over moderate heat until cream is reduced by a quarter. Add champagne and simmer until the sauce has a nice creamy consistency, from 10 to 15 minutes.

6 ■ Return oysters and shrimp to sauce. Add remaining butter and swirl pan until butter is just melted.

7 ■ *To serve:* Cut top of the paper open and fold back. Serve the papillotte sauce separately. (Sauce will hold a couple of hours over simmering water in a double boiler.)

Pompano Grand Duc

SERVES 4

A very elegant rendition of poached pompano in a light champagne mousseline sauce. Garnish with fresh vegetables such as braised Belgian endive or steamed asparagus. For an important dinner, serve it with a marvelous dry white wine like Corton-Charlemagne.

- 8 fillets pompano from four 1-pound pompano (reserve bones for stock)
- 2 tablespoons Creole Seafood Seasoning (page 190)
- 4 cups Fish Stock, preferably made from pompano bones (page 191)
- 4 tablespoons (½ stick) unsalted butter
- 24 shrimp, peeled and deveined
- 24 freshly shucked oysters
- ½ medium onion, minced
- 1 clove of garlic, minced
- 1 teaspoon all-purpose flour
- 2 cups heavy cream
- 1 cup champagne

1 ■ Season fillets with seafood seasoning, put in a sauté pan, cover with stock, and poach over high heat for 1½ minutes. Remove pompano from stock and keep warm. Cook the stock until it is reduced to ½ cup, approximately 1½ hours. Set stock aside.

2 ■ Add butter to the sauté pan and sauté shrimp, oysters, onion, and garlic until the shrimp are pink and the onions transparent. Add flour and stir gently. Add reduced stock and the cream and cook until the sauce is reduced by a third. Add the champagne and stir gently until well blended.

3 ■ Ladle the sauce over the fish and serve immediately.

Redfish with Shrimp

SERVES 4

A simple, light luncheon dish of broiled fish fillets topped with shrimp in a creamy pink shrimp sauce. Redfish is a member of the bass family and one of our local specialties, but you could substitute trout, flounder, or any nonoily fish.

- 16 medium shrimp, peeled and deveined
- 4 tablespoons (½ stick) plus 1 tablespoon unsalted butter
- 1 tablespoon all-purpose flour
- 1 cup Shrimp Stock (page 191)
- 4 teaspoons Creole Seafood Seasoning (page 190)
- 1 cup heavy cream
- 4 redfish fillets, 6 ounces each
- 2 tablespoons (¼ stick) unsalted butter, melted

1 ■ In a skillet sauté shrimp in 4 tablespoons butter until pink. Add flour and stir into butter in pan until well blended. Stir in stock and 2 teaspoons seafood seasoning. Bring to a simmer, stirring, then cook until sauce is reduced by about a third. Add cream and bring to a simmer, stirring. Add 1 tablespoon butter and swirl pan over the heat until butter is just melted and sauce is glazed.

2 ■ Brush redfish with melted butter, sprinkle with 2 teaspoons seafood seasoning, and broil until done.

3 ■ Ladle sauce over the redfish and serve immediately.

Redfish Grieg

SERVES 8

This is an unpretentious dish of baked redfish served with sautéed crab meat and Commander's Creole meunière sauce. Redfish Grieg was invented by one of our waiters for special customers and it became so popular that we put it on the menu for everyone. Take care not to overstir the crab meat or the lumps will break apart.

8 tablespoons (1 stick) unsalted butter, melted
8 fresh redfish fillets (6 ounces each)
2 teaspoons Creole Seafood Seasoning (page 190)
1 cup Seafood Stock (page 191)

Sautéed Crab Meat

8 tablespoons (1 stick) unsalted butter
1 tablespoon Worcestershire sauce
1 teaspoon Creole Seafood Seasoning (page 190)
½ cup minced green onions
1 pound lump crab meat, shells carefully removed

Creole Meunière Sauce (page 194)

1 Preheat oven to 350°.

2 Melt butter in a 13x9x2-inch pan. Sprinkle both sides of the fillets with seafood seasoning and arrange in a single layer in the pan, turning fish once in the melted butter. Add stock to pan.

3 Bake for 10 minutes, or until fish flakes easily. Do *not* overcook. Remove pan from oven and drain off liquid, reserving liquid.

4 Meanwhile, prepare crab meat. In a large skillet melt butter over medium heat. Add Worcestershire sauce, seafood seasoning, and green onions and sauté, stirring, for 1 minute. Remove from heat and add crab meat. Toss gently, trying not to break the lumps. Heat thoroughly and remove from heat.

5 Make Creole meunière sauce.

6 *To serve:* Put 1 fillet on each warmed plate. Top with one eighth of the sautéed crab meat, covering the fillet completely. Spoon 2 to 3 tablespoons meunière sauce over all. Serve immediately.

Redfish with Artichokes and Mushrooms

SERVES 8

Another variation on a theme using our tasty local redfish, this is a light dish of fresh redfish fillets sautéed and served in a lovely vegetable sauce with artichokes and mushrooms. It would be nice for either a luncheon or dinner party served with a chilled Chablis or dry white California wine.

- 2 teaspoons Creole Seafood Seasoning (page 190)
- 1 cup all-purpose flour
- 2 medium eggs, lightly beaten
- 1 cup milk
- 6 redfish fillets, about 6 ounces each
- ½ cup (1 stick) Clarified Butter (page 195) or half oil and half margarine

Artichoke Mushroom Sauce

- ¾ cup (1½ sticks) butter
- 1½ cups cooked sliced artichoke bottoms, fresh or canned
- 1½ cups quartered fresh mushrooms
- 3 cloves of garlic, minced
- 1½ cups minced green onions
- ¾ cup Chablis or other dry white wine
- Juice of ½ lemon
- Pinch of cayenne pepper

Garnish

- Lemon slices
- Sprigs of parsley

1 ■ In a large mixing bowl combine seafood seasoning and flour.

2 ■ Beat eggs and milk lightly until well blended.

3 ■ Dredge fillets in the seasoned flour, then in egg-milk mixture, and again in the flour. Set aside.

4 ■ In a large skillet over medium high heat, heat the clarified butter. Add the fillets and sauté quickly until golden brown on both sides, turning only once. Remove fillets to a warm serving platter and keep warm.

5 ■ *To make the sauce:* Melt half the butter in a sauté pan. Add artichoke bottoms, mushrooms, garlic, green onions, wine, and lemon juice. Simmer, uncovered, until liquid is reduced by one third, or until you have about ½ cup. Add remaining butter and cayenne pepper. Stir gently over low heat until butter is just melted and sauce is creamy.

6 ■ *To serve:* Put a fillet on each warmed plate. Top with sauce and garnish with a slice of lemon and parsley. Serve immediately.

Baked Redfish Court-Bouillon

SERVES 4

A whole baked redfish is served in Commander's special Creole sauce. Fish always has more flavor when it is cooked whole on the bone. For a beautiful presentation, bring out the whole fish on a platter to show to guests before filleting. Serve with rice mixed with chopped parsley.

- 3 tablespoons unsalted butter
- 1 whole fresh redfish, bone in, 3 to 4 pounds, ready to cook
- 8 cups Creole Sauce (page 197)
- 1 lemon, thinly sliced

1 Preheat oven to 350°.

2 Melt butter in a large baking pan and brown fish on both sides. Pour sauce over, arrange lemon slices on top, and bake for 30 minutes.

Redfish in Creole Meunière Sauce

SERVES 6

A simple sautéed fish fillet is prepared in the traditional style. Meunière is the original French fish sauce, but in New Orleans we "Creolize" it with Commander's spicier, well-seasoned version. This recipe works beautifully with either redfish or trout.

- 2 eggs, lightly beaten
- 1 cup milk
- 2 teaspoons Creole Seafood Seasoning (page 190)
- 1 cup flour
- 6 redfish fillets, about 6 ounces each
- ½ cup (1 stick) Clarified Butter (page 195)
- 2 cups Creole Meunière Sauce (page 194)

Garnish

Parsley sprigs
Lemon wedges

1 Combine eggs and milk. Combine seafood seasoning and flour. Dredge fish fillets in the seasoned flour, dip in egg-milk mixture, then dredge again in flour.

2 Sauté fillets quickly in clarified butter in a large skillet over medium heat until crisp and golden on both sides, turning once. Remove fish to a warm serving platter and keep warm until ready to serve.

3 *To serve:* Put a fillet on each warmed plate. Cover trout with the Creole meunière sauce and garnish with parsley and lemon.

Note: The Creole meunière sauce will hold no more than 45 minutes, so use it as soon as possible.

Grilled Redfish

SERVES 8

Also called blackened redfish, this is highly seasoned fish cooked quickly in a very, very hot cast-iron skillet, so that it is black on the outside, sealing in the juices, and white and moist inside. The main secret to its success is a very hot pan. The Creole seafood seasoning is also very important and imparts character to the dish. We serve it on a bed of fresh julienned vegetables with a ramekin of warm lemon butter on the side.

- 8 fresh redfish fillets, about 6 ounces each
- 2 teaspoons Creole Seafood Seasoning (page 190)
- ½ cup (1 stick) unsalted butter, melted
- 1 cup Fish Stock (page 191)

Lemon Butter Sauce

- 4 fresh lemons, peeled
- ¾ pound (3 sticks) unsalted butter

Vegetable Accompaniment

- 1 medium green bell pepper, cut in julienne strips
- 1 small onion, cut in julienne strips
- 1 medium carrot, cut in julienne strips
- 1 stalk celery, cut in julienne strips
- ¼ red cabbage, thinly shredded, or one cup
- ¼ green cabbage, shredded, or one cup
- 4 tablespoons (½ stick) unsalted butter
- 1 teaspoon Creole Seafood Seasoning (page 190)

Garnish

Lemon slices or wedges

1 ■ Pat fish dry and season with seafood seasoning. Brush with melted butter. Refrigerate until 15 minutes before cooking.

2 ■ *To make lemon butter sauce:* Squeeze juice from lemons and mash the pulp in a 2-quart saucepan. Heat juice and pulp to a boil. Add the butter, little by little, whisking after each addition until sauce boils again. When all butter has been added, remove from heat, strain, and hold at room temperature until time to serve.

3 ■ *To cook the fish:* Preheat oven to 350°.

4 ■ Remove fish from refrigerator. Heat a heavy cast-iron skillet until white-hot. Put fish in the skillet. When fish is very brown, *not burned*, turn it over (only once) and continue to cook until brown on other side. Transfer to baking pan. Ladle fish stock over it and finish cooking for 3 to 4 minutes in the oven. Set aside.

5 While fish is baking, cook the vegetables: Put them all into a sauté pan with the butter and seafood seasoning and toss or stir over high heat until vegetables are barely cooked, from 3 to 5 minutes. Vegetables should remain crunchy.

6 *To serve:* Put a portion of the vegetables on each warmed plate. Arrange a fillet of redfish on top of the vegetables and put a small ramekin of warmed lemon-butter sauce on the side. Garnish with lemon slice or wedge.

Redfish au Poivre

SERVES 4

Everyone makes steak au poivre; at Commander's we make redfish au poivre—and it's a knockout! Redfish, a member of the bass species, is a very flavorful fish with a bigger flake and more texture than snapper. If you can't get fresh redfish, you may substitute striped bass, red snapper, or sea trout.

- 4 tablespoons green peppercorns, drained and mashed
- 1 teaspoon black peppercorns, well cracked
- ½ cup brandy
- 1½ cups dry white wine
- ¼ cup cider vinegar
- ⅓ cup Demi-glace (page 193)
- 2 cups heavy cream
- 4 redfish fillets, about 12 ounces each
- 4 tablespoons (½ stick) unsalted butter
- ⅛ teaspoon salt
- 1 teaspoon coarsely ground black pepper

1 In a heavy saucepan combine green and black peppercorns, brandy, 1 cup white wine, and vinegar. Cook over medium heat until all the liquid is evaporated and peppercorns are almost dry, approximately 30 minutes. Add demi-glace and reduce to half its quantity. Add cream and again reduce by half its original quantity. Hold over hot water until ready to serve.

2 Preheat oven to 375°.

3 Dot fillets with butter and sprinkle with salt and pepper. Arrange side by side in an ovenproof dish and cover with the remaining wine. Bake until fish is cooked, about 7 minutes.

4 *To serve:* Pour a spoonful of the sauce on each warmed serving plate and arrange a fillet on top.

Creole Coulibiac of Redfish

SERVES 6

The chef at our Mr. B's Restaurant in the French Quarter created this Creole coulibiac by taking the classic French recipe and changing the seasoning to bring it up to Haute Creole. Redfish fillets are wrapped in a mushroom duxelles and rice pilaf and encased in a brioche shell, making it an elegant party dish. We serve it at both lunch and dinner with a mild sauce of beurre fondu. A full-bodied California Chardonnay wine such as Acacia would be a perfect complement.

- 2 redfish fillets, each about 1 pound
- Salt and cayenne pepper

Mushroom Duxelles

- 1 pound mushrooms
- 6 shallots
- 1 clove of garlic
- 1 tablespoon unsalted butter
- ½ teaspoon chopped tarragon
- ½ teaspoon thyme
- ½ teaspoon crushed black pepper
- ¼ cup dry white wine
- ¼ cup heavy cream

Pilaf

- ½ medium onion, diced
- 2 stalks celery, finely chopped
- 2 tablespoons (¼ stick) unsalted butter
- 1 cup converted rice
- 2 cups Chicken Stock (page 192), heated
- ¼ cup finely chopped green onions
- Salt, freshly ground black pepper, and Worcestershire sauce to taste

Beurre Fondu

- 2 tablespoons heavy cream
- 1 pound (4 sticks) cold butter, cut into bits
- Juice of 1 lemon
- Freshly ground black pepper

- 2 hard-cooked eggs, finely chopped
- 2 tablespoons chopped fresh parsley
- Salt and freshly ground black pepper
- 1½ pounds unsweetened brioche dough, frozen or homemade
- 1 egg, lightly beaten
- ½ cup milk

1 Trim the redfish fillets so they are 2 inches wide, reserving any trimmings. Season well with salt and cayenne pepper. Cook fillets in a heavy very hot skillet in a very little oil, until each side is seared but dish is not cooked. Set aside.

2 *To make the duxelles:* Grind mushrooms with fine blade of a grinder or with a food processor. Finely dice shallots and garlic and sauté in 1 tablespoon butter. Add mushrooms, herbs, pepper, and wine and simmer until all juices have been reduced, leaving only moist mushrooms, about 20 minutes. Correct seasoning and blend in the cream. Set aside.

3 *To make the pilaf:* In a heavy saucepan sauté onion and celery in 1 tablespoon butter until onion is transparent. Add rice and remaining butter. Stir until rice is well coated with butter. Add hot stock, green onions, and salt, pepper, and Worcestershire sauce. Bring to a boil, cover tightly, and cook over low heat (or bake in a 350° oven) until rice is tender and liquid is absorbed, 12 to 20 minutes. Set aside.

4 *To make a beurre fondu:* In a saucepan heat cream to a boil. Gradually whisk in butter bit by bit until all is incorporated and the sauce is the consistency of heavy cream. Remove from heat. Whisk in lemon juice and pepper to taste. Set aside.

5 Preheat oven to 375°.

6 Combine chopped eggs, parsley, salt and pepper. Set aside.

7 Roll out brioche dough ¼ inch thick in a rectangle 5x12 inches. Trim, saving trimming for decoration on top.

8 Lengthwise along center of dough place a band of pilaf 2 inches wide and coming to within 2 inches of the ends of the dough, using about half the pilaf. Put a fillet on top of the rice and use trimming if necessary to completely cover the pilaf. Cover the fillet with half the duxelles and sprinkle with half the chopped egg mixture. Repeat the procedure so there are two layers of all the ingredients.

9 Combine egg and milk. Fold dough over the fish on each side to meet on top. Trim excess, brush with egg-milk mixture, and press down ends to seal; trim excess. Cut three holes about ½ inch in diameter for vents in top of the coulibiac and decorate with the remaining dough, cut into flower-petal shapes and leaves. Brush the entire coulibiac with egg mixture and bake for 25 minutes. During the baking period, pour beurre fondu into the vent holes two or three times, reserving enough to serve with the coulibiac.

10 *To serve:* Remove coulibiac from oven and let rest for 10 minutes. Then slice 1 inch thick and serve with a spoonful of the sauce.

Note: The beurre fondu sauce is also elegant on hot broiled clams.

Whole Redfish Stuffed with Seafood Mousse

SERVES 4

A new, elegant, and light dish, whole redfish stuffed with seafood mousse is perfect for an important dinner when you want to serve something different and dramatic. Not a typical frothy mousse, the seafood stuffing of puréed fish fillet and shrimp bound with eggs and cream is more highly seasoned (with Louisiana Red Hot Sauce) and has a hearty texture and lots of flavor. You can make this either with individual small fish or 1 large fish sliced vertically into round steaks for a pretty presentation. You can also add fresh herbs such as dill, tarragon, or basil to the mousse mixture.

- 1 whole redfish, about 2 to 2½ pounds, completely boned
- Juice of ½ lemon
- Salt and freshly ground black pepper

Seafood Mousse

- ½ pound boneless redfish fillet
- ½ pound shrimp, peeled and deveined
- ¼ medium onion
- 1 clove of garlic
- 2 teaspoons Louisiana Red Hot Sauce
- Salt and freshly ground black pepper
- 1 tablespoon finely chopped green onions
- 1 cup heavy cream
- 3 egg whites, fork-whipped until frothy
- 2 cups Fish Stock (page 191) or court-bouillon

1 ■ Rinse inside of redfish, pat dry, and rub with lemon juice and salt and pepper to taste.

2 ■ *To make the mousse:* Grind fillet, shrimp, onion, and garlic with fine blade of a meat grinder, or use a food processor. Put in a chilled electric mixer bowl and season with hot sauce, salt and pepper, and green onion. Gradually beat in half the cream. Then put mixer bowl in a larger bowl filled with ice. With a wooden spoon gradually work the egg whites and remaining cream into the fish mixture. Correct seasoning.

3 ■ Preheat oven to 350°.

4 ■ Stuff the redfish with the mousse mixture, allowing for expansion. Put the stuffed fish in a roasting pan with the stock and bake for 35 minutes.

5 ■ *To serve:* Slice the fish crosswise entirely through body and stuffing for 4 portions.

Redfish Orleans

SERVES 4 TO 6

A new favorite, redfish Orleans was created by New Orleans–born chef Floyd Bealer, who has worked with us for some twenty-five years. Redfish fillets are stuffed with sautéed julienned carrots, onions, and celery and baked with leeks, port wine, and sherry. The crowning sauce is a reduction of the pan juices finished with a swirl of butter.

1 cup fine julienne-cut carrots
1 cup fine julienne-cut onions
1 cup fine julienne-cut celery
2 cloves of garlic, minced
½ pound (2 sticks) unsalted butter
6 redfish fillets, about 4 ounces each
Salt and freshly ground black pepper to taste
1 cup chopped white portion of leeks
½ cup port
½ cup sherry
Salt and freshly ground black pepper

Garnish

Watercress

1 Preheat oven to 350°.

2 Sauté carrots, onions, celery, and garlic in half the butter until tender.

3 Season fish fillets with salt and pepper, slice each in half lengthwise to create a "pocket," and fill with the cooked vegetables. Arrange on a bed of chopped leeks in a baking pan. Add port and sherry, cover with aluminum foil, and bake for 20 minutes.

4 When fish is cooked, transfer from baking pan to warm platter and keep warm. Cook liquid remaining in pan over direct heat until reduced by one quarter. Strain sauce into a saucepan. Gradually whisk in remaining butter and salt and pepper to taste.

5 Ladle the creamy sauce onto warmed plates. Put a stuffed fillet on top of the sauce and garnish with watercress.

Oyster and Artichoke Casserole

SERVES 4

An old New Orleans dish, this classic combination of briny oysters and sweet artichoke hearts served in individual casseroles is especially satisfying and soothing on a cold day. It may be served as an appetizer in a small ramekin or as a main course on a bed of rice, accompanied by hot, crispy French bread.

- 5 tablespoons unsalted butter
- 4 tablespoons all-purpose flour
- 40 oysters, shucked
- 2 cups oyster liquor (see footnote page 23)
- 2 bay leaves
- ¼ teaspoon thyme
- 2 cups coarsely chopped green onions
- 12 cooked artichoke hearts (fresh or canned), quartered
- Salt and freshly ground black pepper
- ½ cup fresh bread crumbs
- ½ cup freshly grated Parmesan cheese

1 ■ Melt 4 tablespoons butter in a small saucepan. Add flour and stir over moderate heat until the roux is smooth and bubbling and a golden color. Set aside.

2 ■ Preheat oven to 350°.

3 ■ Put oysters, oyster liquor, bay leaves, and thyme in a sauté pan. Bring liquor to a simmer and poach oysters until edges begin to curl. Remove oysters to individual casseroles, allowing 10 oysters per casserole. Continue to cook the liquor until it is reduced to about 1½ cups. Add the roux and blend in thoroughly. Add green onions, artichokes, and salt and pepper to taste. Remove sauté pan from heat and whisk in the remaining butter. Spoon sauce over the oysters.

4 ■ Combine bread crumbs and cheese. Sprinkle over oysters in casseroles and bake until topping in the casseroles is golden brown, about 10 minutes. Serve immediately.

Oyster Patties

SERVES 8

This dish was originally inspired by a classic Cajun recipe for hearty, highly seasoned oyster patty cakes. We adapted it to Haute Creole by changing the filling to a light and elegant oyster–onion–green onion mixture and serving it in puff pastry shells. It is nice for a luncheon, or, using small pastry shells, for cocktails, as bite-size hors d'oeuvres.

- 1 large onion, finely chopped
- 8 tablespoons (1 stick) unsalted butter
- 6 green onions, finely chopped
- 7 tablespoons all-purpose flour
- 1 quart oyster liquor (see footnote page 23)
- 4 dozen medium oysters, shucked
- Juice of ½ lemon
- 3 tablespoons finely chopped parsley
- Salt and freshly ground black pepper
- 8 large puff pastry shells, baked

1 Sauté onion in butter until soft. Add green onions and cook until soft but not brown. Add flour and stir until well blended with the butter. Gradually stir in as much of the oyster liquor as needed to make a very thick, well-blended sauce. You may need to use it all.

2 Add oysters and lemon juice and stir gently. Simmer for 10 minutes. Add parsley and correct seasoning to taste.

3 Preheat oven to 370°.

4 Thirty minutes before you are ready to serve, spoon oyster mixture into the patty shells, put shells on a baking sheet, and bake for 30 minutes.

Note: If you wish to serve this dish as a cocktail appetizer, use very small, cocktail-size puff pastry shells. Recipe will make 24.

Oysters en Brochette

SERVES 4

Easy, delicious, and very versatile, oysters en brochette can be served as a main dish for lunch or dinner or as an appetizer. Oysters are wrapped in bacon and skewered, lightly dusted with flour and seafood seasoning, and deep-fried. Be careful not to overcook the oysters or they will dry out. Serve with spicy Creole dipping sauce on the side.

- Ingredients for 1 cup Creole Meunière Sauce (page 194)
- 32 medium oysters, freshly shucked
- 16 slices bacon, halved crosswise
- 1½ cups all-purpose flour
- 2 tablespoons Creole Seafood Seasoning (page 190)
- Oil for frying

1 Prepare Creole meunière sauce and set aside. It will keep for 45 minutes.

2 Roll each oyster in ½ slice bacon and place on a toothpick or skewer.

3 In a large mixing bowl, combine flour and seafood seasoning. Dredge the skewered oysters and bacon with seasoned flour.

4 Heat 1 inch of oil in a shallow frypan until hot but not smoking, about 350°. Fry oysters until bacon is brown and crisp. Drain on paper towel.

5 Serve 8 oysters per person, with the sauce on the side.

Jambalaya

SERVES 6

New Orleans's version of Spanish paella, jambalaya is a Cajun recipe for country-style "pot cooking" at its best. Every cook and every home has its own jambalaya recipe. Shrimp Creole Sauce (page 92) is good over the jambalaya.

- 1/4 cup Clarified Butter (page 195)
- 1 onion, coarsely chopped
- 1 green bell pepper, coarsely chopped
- 3 ribs celery, coarsely chopped
- 5 cloves of garlic, minced
- 1 1/2 pounds shrimp, peeled and deveined
- 1 1/2 pounds boneless, skinless chicken, cut into 1 1/2-inch cubes
- 3 bay leaves
- 1/2 teaspoon thyme
- 1/4 teaspoon paprika
- 2 28-ounce cans stewed tomatoes
- 1 cup Chicken Stock (page 192)
- 3 teaspoons Louisiana Red Hot Sauce
- 1/4 cup Worcestershire sauce
- 1/2 pound andouille sausage or other spicy sausage like kielbasa, sliced 1/4 inch thick
- 1/2 pound smoked ham, cut into 1/2-inch cubes
- 1/2 pound crawfish tails, peeled
- 1 bunch green onions, coarsely chopped
- Salt
- 3 cups long-grained rice

1 Heat butter in an uncovered heavy-bottomed pot or kettle. Add vegetables and garlic and sauté, stirring, for 5 minutes. Add shrimp, chicken, bay leaves, and thyme and continue to cook over medium heat until chicken becomes white and shrimp are pink, about 10 to 15 minutes.

2 Add paprika and stir thoroughly to mix well with other ingredients. Add tomatoes, stock, hot sauce, and Worcestershire sauce. Mix well.

3 Add sausage and ham. Stir well. Add crawfish tails and cook over moderate heat until liquid returns to a boil. Add green onions, salt to taste, and rice. Cook over low heat for 30 minutes.

New Orleans Bouillabaisse

SERVES 10 TO 12

New Orleans bouillabaisse is a perfect example of the way Creole cuisine has evolved from the original French provincial cooking. A classic bouillabaisse is in a clear saffron broth, while a New Orleans bouillabaisse is a thicker stew-type dish with our special Creole seasonings and all local fish and shellfish. You can substitute any fresh regional fish.

- 4 tablespoons (½ stick) unsalted butter
- 6 tablespoons olive oil
- 2 large white onions, finely chopped
- 6 green onions, finely chopped
- 3 stalks celery, finely chopped
- 3 cloves of garlic, finely chopped
- 2 tablespoons all-purpose flour
- 4 tomatoes, peeled and chopped
- 1½ teaspoons salt
- 1 teaspoon cayenne pepper
- ½ teaspoon freshly ground black pepper
- 1 teaspoon thyme
- ¼ teaspoon ground allspice
- ¼ teaspoon ground cloves
- 1 teaspoon chili powder
- 1 quart Fish Stock (page 191), strained and reduced by half
- 3 cups Chicken Stock (page 192)
- 4 pounds fish fillets (use head and bones for fish stock)
- Salt and freshly ground black pepper
- 1 pound shrimp, peeled and deveined
- 2 dozen oysters, freshly shucked
- 1 cup oyster liquor (see footnote page 23)
- 1 pound crawfish tails, peeled
- 1 pound crab meat from claws
- 6 small soft-shell crabs, sautéed in butter and halved
- ½ cup dry white wine
- Good pinch of saffron threads
- 1 tablespoon minced parsley
- 12 slices toasted French bread

Garnish

Lemon slices

1 Preheat oven to 350°.

2 Melt butter in a very large heavy pot or kettle. Add olive oil and sauté onions, green onions, celery, and garlic over low heat for 6 to 8 minutes. Stir in flour and cook 5 minutes longer, stirring occasionally. Add tomatoes, salt, cayenne, black pepper, thyme, allspice, cloves, chili powder, fish stock, and chicken stock. Bring to a boil, lower heat to a simmer, and cook for 25 minutes.

3 Meanwhile, rub fillets with salt and black pepper and bake for 15 minutes.

4 When soup has finished cooking, add shrimp, oysters and oyster liquor, crawfish, crab meat, and crabs. Cook for 5 minutes. Then add wine, saffron, and parsley. Add the baked fish fillets and cook 5 minutes longer, correcting the seasoning as needed.

5 *To serve:* Put a slice of toasted French bread in bottom of each soup bowl, place half a soft-shell crab on top, and fill the bowl with the soup. Garnish with lemon slices.

Deep-Fried Catfish

SERVES 4

Everyone in New Orleans adores catfish, but we had always thought it too ordinary for the restaurant. Recently, however, luncheon chef Floyd Bealer created this special recipe and it's become very popular—a country dish that might be described as "soul food." The catfish, which is a firm, flaky fish, is marinated overnight, then battered in yellow cornmeal and seafood seasoning, deep-fried for 3 or 4 minutes, and served with an herbal Creole mustard sauce on the side. It's really crisp outside and moist inside.

- ½ cup Creole or Dijon mustard
- ¼ cup buttermilk
- 1 teaspoon Creole Seafood Seasoning (page 190)
- Juice of 2 lemons
- 8 catfish fillets, 4 ounces each

Creole Mustard Sauce with Herbs

- 1 cup Homemade Mayonnaise (page 66)
- 3 tablespoons Creole or Dijon mustard
- ⅓ tablespoon thyme
- ⅓ tablespoon oregano
- ⅓ tablespoon finely chopped dill
- Juice of 1 lemon

- ½ cup yellow cornmeal seasoned with Creole seafood seasoning
- Shortening for frying

1 Combine mustard, buttermilk, seafood seasoning, and lemon juice in a mixing bowl and marinate the catfish fillets overnight.

2 Combine all ingredients for the sauce.

3 Remove fillets, pat dry, and roll in cornmeal. Fry in shortening heated to 350° for 3 to 4 minutes, or until nicely brown on both sides. Serve with sauce.

Charcoaled Flounder with Beurre Blanc

SERVES 4

A simple outdoors dish, perfect for summer entertaining, whole flounder is seasoned with fresh herbs, lightly coated with flour and oil, sautéed, and grilled over a hot charcoal or wood fire. If making this indoors, you can use the broiler. Cook only 2 minutes on each side, as flounder is a delicate fish; be careful not to overcook it, or it will become dry. Serve with our special Creole beurre blanc and seasonal vegetables.

- 4 small whole flounder, 10 to 12 ounces each, head and fins removed
- Thyme, cayenne pepper, salt, and freshly ground black pepper
- 1 cup all-purpose flour
- ¼ cup oil

Creole Beurre Blanc

- ½ cup chopped shallots
- 2 cloves of garlic, chopped
- 1 teaspoon crushed black pepper
- 1 tomato (Creole or beefsteak), peeled, seeded, and diced
- ½ cup dry white wine
- ¼ cup white wine vinegar
- 2 tablespoons heavy cream
- 1 teaspoon chopped tarragon
- 1 tablespoon finely sliced green onions
- 1¼ pounds (5 sticks) cold unsalted butter, cut into bits
- Salt, cayenne pepper, Worcestershire sauce, and lemon juice

Garnish

- Parsley sprigs

1 Make 2 small incisions in each side of the fish and rub with thyme, cayenne pepper, salt, and black pepper to taste. Dredge the fish lightly with flour and arrange side by side in a pan with oil to barely coat the fish.

2 Prepare a very hot charcoal or wood fire, or preheat broiler to very hot. Preheat oven to 300°.

3 Arrange fish on the grill, turning to mark each side, then cook until fish flakes with a fork, about 2 minutes per side.

4 *To make Creole beurre blanc:* Put shallots, garlic, black pepper, tomato, wine, and vinegar in saucepan and reduce liquid over high heat until completely evaporated and only the moist shallot mixture remains. Remove from heat and add cream, tarragon, and green onions. Begin to whisk in the butter, piece by piece, moving pan on and off heat to keep temperature from getting too hot or too cool. When all butter is whisked in the sauce should be the consistency of hollandaise. Adjust seasoning with salt, cayenne pepper, Worcestershire sauce, and lemon juice to taste.

5 *To serve:* Pour some sauce on each warmed plate. Put a fish on top and garnish with parsley. Serve additional sauce on the side.

Stuffed Flounder

SERVES 4

Light and elegant, this new recipe for flounder stuffed with seafood replaced the old heavy version and becomes Haute Creole. Flounder is one of the area's greatest fish, and, we believe, superior in taste to sole. You can make the mushroom and crab meat filling ahead—for instance, in the morning for use that evening. When adding the fresh lump crab meat be careful to toss it gently so that the crab remains in large tasty chunks. Use only fresh flounder and fresh crab. If flounder is unavailable, substitute sole.

- 4 whole flounder, 1 pound each
- 8 tablespoons (1 stick) unsalted butter
- 2 ounces shallots (4 medium), finely chopped
- 1 teaspoon finely chopped parsley
- 1 pound fresh mushrooms, sliced
- ½ cup Chablis
- 2 cups heavy cream
- ½ pound fresh lump crab meat, shells carefully removed
- ½ teaspoon Creole Seafood Seasoning (page 190)
- Creole Beurre Blanc (page 118)

1 Clean and wash fish. Remove head and side bones, or have fishmonger do it. Cut a deep slit down each side of backbone and remove.

2 *To make the stuffing:* Melt half the butter in a saucepan. Add shallots, parsley, and mushrooms and sauté for 2 minutes, stirring. Add wine and cream and reduce until sauce is thickened and creamy. Add crab meat and seafood seasoning and stir gently, being careful not to break up the lumps.

3 Preheat oven to 350°.

4 Butter a baking sheet generously with remaining butter and arrange the flounder on it. Open fish and fill with the stuffing. Close fish and bake for 15 to 20 minutes.

5 Serve with beurre blanc.

Chicken and Game

Louisiana is one of the great game areas of the world because of its rich marshlands. Our local birds are so remarkable that Audubon devoted his life to their study; his lavishly illustrated book on the birds of Louisiana is one of the most beautiful ever produced about birds.

New Orleans is a big duck-hunting town. The season gets under way around Thanksgiving and runs through mid-January. All the members of the Brennan family hunt. Even Dick's children go duck hunting by themselves, and when they bring back their catch the butcher here shows them how to prepare the ducks for roasting. At the restaurant we buy our ducks commercially from Wisconsin (it is against the law to sell the game you catch), but often customers will bring us freshly caught wild game birds to prepare in a special way for them. Recently a good client celebrated his birthday by having a party for twenty friends and brought us wonderful wild mallard ducks the day before. We prepared a special game menu that included pressed duck—an elegant and elaborate dish that is perfect for special occasions. In a dramatic presentation tableside we used a beautiful old-fashioned silver duck press to squeeze out the bones and extract every last drop of the birds' natural juices—the essence of the wild-duck flavor.

There are many varieties of wild duck in Louisiana: pintail, mallard, teal, and widgeon are favored by epicureans. We also have wild squab or pigeonneau, tiny baby quail, and Louisiana goose.

Game birds should be prepared by larding or wrapping in bacon before slow roasting on a low fire. Baste frequently, being careful not to overcook, and finish the birds off on the grill or broiler. They can be cooked plain, roasted or broiled, as well as with fancy French sauces, in styles suiting the taste of the plebeian farmer as well as the patrician banker. Generally, small birds like squab and quail can be split down the center, butterflied, and broiled or grilled; larger birds such as duck, pheasant, and turkey are usually roasted. The wonderful wild-game flavor is more apparent when the birds are broiled or roasted. Whether you are shooting your supper or buying the birds, allow 1 whole small bird, half a larger bird, or about 1 pound per person.

If you cannot get fresh *wild* game for these recipes, you can use chicken, Rock Cornish hen, and farm-raised quail, pheasant, turkey, and duck with excellent results.

Traditional accompaniments include Southern sweet potatoes, simply roasted in the pan with the bird, or mixed with pecans, brown sugar, and spices, as in our own divine yams Richard. "Dirty" rice, that traditional Cajun dish made with chicken livers and gizzards, vegetables, and spices, is wonderful with quail, as well as other game birds. And our grand roast goose has the traditional German accompaniment of red cabbage and apples.

On special occasions and holidays such as Christmas we serve roast turkey with a classic New Orleans oyster dressing and our own cranberry-orange relish, marinated in rum and Grand Marnier.

In general, fat game, such as goose, combines well with lean ingredients, and game with little fat, such as turkey, requires richer accompaniments.

Chapter opening illustration: *The rich Louisiana marshlands are filled with many varieties of wild game birds, and duck hunting is very popular.*

Breasts of Chicken Tarragon

SERVES 4

Scallops of tender boneless chicken breasts are gently sautéed and served with a white wine sauce flavored with tarragon. This is a quick and simple dish that raises everyday chicken to Haute Creole. If you don't have veal stock you can substitute chicken stock.

- 4 whole chicken breasts, boned and skinned
- Salt and freshly ground black pepper
- 3 tablespoons Clarified Butter (page 195)
- All-purpose flour for dredging
- ½ cup dry white wine
- ½ cup Veal Stock (page 192)
- 1 tablespoon chopped tarragon
- 4 tablespoons (½ stick) unsalted butter

1 ■ Cut chicken breasts in half and put the 8 pieces of chicken between parchment or waxed paper and pound with the flat side of a meat tenderizer until very thin. Sprinkle with salt and pepper to taste and dredge lightly in flour. Sauté in clarified butter in a heavy skillet until just lightly browned, 2 minutes per side. Remove breasts to a warm serving platter.

2 ■ Drain excess butter from pan and add wine. Cook over moderate heat, stirring in all the nice brown bits of chicken glaze adhering to bottom and sides of pan. Boil wine rapidly until reduced by half. Add stock and again reduce by half. Add tarragon, simmer 1 minute, then swirl in pieces of butter until butter is just melted. Do not let sauce boil.

3 ■ Adjust seasoning and pour sauce over chicken breasts.

Chicken Pontalba

SERVES 4

Created by Chef Paul Blangé in the early days of Brennan's, this dish was named after the beautiful Baroness Pontalba, who came to New Orleans in the 1700s. Boneless breast of baked chicken is presented on a bed of seasoned vegetables mixed with crisp fried potatoes and ham, all topped with a rich, buttery béarnaise. The vegetable-ham base also makes an excellent filling for an omelet topped with béarnaise.

- 10 tablespoons (1½ sticks) unsalted butter
- 2 whole chicken breasts, halved and boned
- 8 cloves of garlic, minced
- 2 cups diced boiled ham
- 12 fresh mushrooms, diced
- 16 green onion tops, coarsely chopped
- 2 teaspoons Creole Meat Seasoning (page 190)
- ¼ cup dry white wine
- 2 cups finely diced potatoes
- Oil for frying
- 8 tablespoons Béarnaise Sauce (page 196)

1 Preheat oven to 400°.

2 Melt 6 tablespoons butter in a shallow baking pan. Dip chicken breasts in butter, coating them on all sides, arrange in the pan, and bake until tender and lightly browned, 10 to 15 minutes. Set aside and keep warm until ready to serve.

3 Heat remaining butter in a sauté pan and sauté garlic, ham, mushrooms, green onions, and meat seasoning until vegetables are slightly cooked. Add wine and simmer gently to slightly reduce the quantity of the sauce.

4 Meanwhile, fry the diced potatoes in oil heated to 365°. Remove with a slotted spoon when potatoes are golden and crisp and drain on paper towel.

5 *To serve:* Add the fried potatoes to the vegetable-wine mixture and toss lightly. Put a spoonful on each plate and top with half a chicken breast. Top each portion with 2 tablespoons béarnaise sauce and serve immediately.

Chicken Margaux

SERVES 4

A timeless recipe, chicken Margaux is an impressive and easy dish to make. Fry boneless chicken breasts first and set aside while making the sauce, a simple reduction of stock and red wine with mushrooms, green onions, and artichoke hearts. You can also substitute fresh wild mushrooms for special effect. Try this dish with a good claret.

- 4 whole chicken breasts, halved, boned, and skinned
- Creole Meat Seasoning (page 190)
- ½ cup vegetable oil
- 8 tablespoons all-purpose flour
- 2 cups Chicken Stock (page 192)
- ½ cup dry red wine
- 1 cup fresh sliced mushrooms
- 1 cup coarsely chopped green onions
- ½ cup quartered cooked artichoke hearts, fresh or canned
- Salt and freshly ground black pepper
- 1 cup raw rice

1 ■ Sprinkle chicken with meat seasoning. In a 3-quart heavy saucepan heat oil and fry chicken until golden brown on all sides. Remove chicken and set aside.

2 ■ Add flour to the hot oil and stir until flour and oil are well mixed. Add stock, whisking constantly. Reduce heat to a simmer. Add wine and continue to stir until sauce comes to a boil. Reduce heat and let sauce simmer until reduced to about 1½ cups, about 5 minutes.

3 ■ Add mushrooms, green onions, and artichoke hearts. Return chicken to the sauce and simmer for 15 minutes. Correct seasoning with salt and pepper to taste and continue to simmer until chicken is cooked and tender, about 15 to 20 minutes more.

4 ■ Meanwhile, cook rice according to package directions, using the least amount of water possible. When the rice is cooked there should be no water left in the saucepan. Fluff rice with a fork.

5 ■ Spoon a pile of hot fluffy rice onto each warmed plate and serve the chicken on top.

Crêpes Claire

SERVES 2

Named after our brother John's wife, Claire, this has become a very popular, light "ladies' luncheon" dish. It is also ideal for parties, because the crêpes and filling can be made ahead and assembled at the last minute. The crêpes are filled with diced cooked white meat of chicken (this is a good way to use up leftover roast or baked chicken), crisp crumbled bacon, mushrooms, and green onions blended in a béchamel sauce, and garnished with a red ripe grilled tomato.

- 1 whole chicken breast, skinned and boned
- 3 slices bacon
- ¼ cup coarsely chopped green onions
- ¼ cup sliced fresh mushrooms
- 1 tablespoon unsalted butter
- 1 cup Béchamel Sauce (page 198)
- 1 tomato
- Freshly grated Parmesan cheese
- 2 Crêpes (page 164)

1 Broil chicken breast until tender. Cool, then cut meat into ½-inch cubes and set aside.

2 Fry or broil the bacon until crisp. Drain on paper towel. Crumble and set aside.

3 Sauté green onions and mushrooms in butter until tender. Add chicken pieces and bacon and mix gently. Add sauce and stir until well blended and hot.

4 Cut tomato in half, sprinkle lightly with cheese, and broil until cheese is lightly browned, about 5 minutes.

5 *To serve:* Put a crêpe on a warmed plate, pale side up. Spoon a quarter of the chicken mixture on half the crêpe, fold crêpe over, and top with another quarter of the chicken mixture. Garnish with half a grilled tomato and serve immediately.

Pressed Duck

SERVES 4 TO 6

The most regal of all duck dishes, pressed duck makes a fabulous presentation. You must, however, have a duck press (best would be a beautiful silver one). Very popular at duck-hunting season, around Thanksgiving, this elaborate and elegant dish should ideally be made when someone has given you a gift of a brace of fresh wild ducks. The best kind of ducks to use are 1- to 1½-pound mallards.

- 2 ducklings, about 5 pounds each
- 2 tablespoons Creole Meat Seasoning (page 190)
- 2 carrots, washed and coarsely cut
- 2 cups sliced celery with some of the leaves
- ½ celery root, peeled and sliced
- 2 medium onions, quartered
- 6 cloves of garlic
- 1 tablespoon coarsely ground black pepper
- 4 sage leaves
- 1 sprig rosemary
- 1 cup dry red wine
- 2 tablespoons port
- 4 tablespoons (½ stick) unsalted butter

1 ■ Preheat oven to 300°.

2 ■ Cut wing tips from duckling. Reserve wing tips and neck bones. Season ducks inside and out with meat seasoning.

3 ■ Put vegetables, garlic, and bones (wing tips and necks) with pepper and herbs in roasting pan. Put ducklings on top. Roast in oven for about 1½ hours. Ducklings should be rare; the juices that run from thick part of the thigh when pricked with a fork should be slightly red or pink in color.

4 ■ Remove ducklings from pan and carefully remove the skin, keeping it in one piece if possible. Working from a slit down center back, roll and lift the skin first from one side and then from the other, cutting it loose from the meat when necessary with a sharp knife. Then remove breast meat and flesh from legs, roll the meat in the duck skin, and keep warm.

5 ■ Put the remaining carcass in the duck press and extract as much juice as possible. Then put all the vegetables and bones from the roasting pan in the press and press lightly. Combine the liquids and reserve.

6 ■ Add red wine and port to the drippings in the roasting pan. Add duck liquids and cook rapidly, stirring constantly, until liquid is reduced by half. Whisk in butter, a little at a time, without letting the sauce boil.

7 ■ Cut duck meat into slices and spoon sauce over. Serve immediately.

Duck Jambalaya

SERVES 6

This is a wonderful dish for luncheons or parties because you can stretch it with rice if you don't know how many people are coming. We sometimes serve it at home after football games or Mardi Gras parades. You can make it 2 or 3 hours ahead and keep it covered in a warm oven. You need a big heavy-bottomed iron skillet, 2 to 3 inches deep, to cook in and a pretty chafing dish to serve it—or a gorgeous copper pot to do both.

We serve this Creole classic in the fall and winter because it is a hearty meal by itself, accompanied by a simple fresh green salad and a nice claret.

- ¼ cup Clarified Butter (page 195)
- 1 onion, coarsely chopped
- 1 green bell pepper, coarsely chopped
- 3 stalks celery, coarsely chopped
- 5 cloves of garlic, minced
- 1 fresh duck (about 5 pounds), skinned and boned
- 3 bay leaves
- ½ teaspoon thyme
- ¼ cup paprika
- 2 cans tomatoes (1 pound 12 ounces each), including liquid
- 2 cups Duck Stock (page 192)
- 1 tablespoon Louisiana Red Hot Sauce
- ¼ cup Worcestershire sauce
- 1 bunch green onions, coarsely chopped
- Salt to taste
- 3 cups long-grain rice

1 Melt butter in a heavy thick-bottomed pot. Add vegetables and garlic, and sauté for 5 minutes, stirring frequently.

2 Cut the duck meat into large dice and add to the vegetables, along with bay leaves and thyme. Cook over medium heat for 10 to 15 minutes. Add paprika and stir thoroughly to mix with other ingredients. Add tomatoes, stock, hot sauce, and Worcestershire sauce and mix well. Lower heat, cover, and cook until duck is tender, about 1 hour longer.

3 Half an hour before serving time, add green onions and bring liquid to a boil. Adjust salt and make sure there is enough liquid to cook the rice —at least 4 cups. Stir in rice and cook over low heat for 30 minutes longer, stirring occasionally.

Roast Duck with Green Peppercorns

SERVES 4 TO 6

A relatively new "Creolized" version of the French classic, Commander's recipe adds Creole meat seasoning, soy sauce, garlic, onions, and fresh herbs to the basic reduction of duck stock, cream, and peppercorns. We like it accompanied by braised Belgian endive.

2 ducks, about 5 pounds each
2 tablespoons Creole Meat Seasoning (page 190)
2 carrots, scraped and coarsely cut
½ celery root, peeled and coarsely cut
2 medium onions, halved
6 cloves of garlic
1 sprig rosemary
4 sage leaves
3 cups Chablis
2 tablespoons soy sauce
1 cup vegetable oil for frying
1 tablespoon crushed black peppercorns
2 cups heavy cream
2 tablespoons green peppercorns, drained

1 Preheat oven to 300°.

2 Cut wing tips from ducks. Reserve wing tips and neck bones. Season ducks inside and out with meat seasoning.

3 Arrange vegetables, garlic, and wing tips and neck bones in roasting pan and add herbs. Put ducks on this savory bed and roast for 45 minutes. Add wine and soy sauce to roasting pan. Cover with aluminum foil and roast for another hour.

4 Slice duck meat from bones and keep warm. Return bones to roasting pan and continue to cook for a few minutes. Then strain off the stock into a heavy saucepan, pressing the vegetables to extract as much juice as possible. Skim fat off surface of stock and cook stock over medium heat until reduced by three quarters and nicely glazed.

5 Peel back skin from the ducks and scrape off and discard duck fat adhering to the underside. Cut legs and thighs into 2 pieces.

6 Cut breast skin lengthwise, then cut skins in julienne strips and deep-fry in hot oil until crisp. Drain on paper towels. Sprinkle lightly with crushed black peppercorns.

7 Bring cream to a boil in a small saucepan. Add green peppercorns and beat in the duck glaze. Keep warm until ready to serve.

8 *To serve:* Pour the sauce over the ducks and garnish with crisply fried skin.

Duck and Fettuccine

SERVES 6

New Orleans has a large Italian population, and this dish demonstrates how Creole and Italian cuisines can be blended harmoniously. It is a perfect way to use leftover roast duck, sliced in slivers the size of your little finger. You can reduce the stock while the fettuccine is cooking, taking care not to overcook it; the pasta should be not quite al dente, *for it will finish cooking in the sauce.*

- 1 5-pound domestic duckling, roasted, or about 6 cups leftover duck meat
- 8 tablespoons (1 stick) unsalted butter
- 8 cloves of garlic, peeled and minced
- 4 tomatoes, peeled, seeded, and diced
- 2 cups coarsely chopped green onions
- 8 large fresh mushrooms, sliced
- 2 teaspoons Creole Meat Seasoning (page 190)
- 2 cups Duck or Beef Stock (page 192)
- 1 pound fettuccine, cooked until barely *al dente* and rinsed

1 Remove skin from duckling; slice the meat from the bones and set aside.

2 Melt butter in a large sauté pan or skillet. Add garlic, tomatoes, green onions, mushrooms, meat seasoning, and duck meat. Stir gently over low heat until vegetables are wilted. Add stock, bring to a boil, and simmer until liquid is reduced by about a third.

3 Add the cooked noodles and bring sauce back to a simmer, spooning the sauce constantly over the noodles until they are heated through and have finished cooking. They should be steaming hot but still slightly *al dente.*

4 Serve immediately.

Brandied Crisp Roast Duck with Peaches

SERVES 8

Duck has traditionally been roasted and served with a sweet fruit sauce. The rich, syrupy peach sauce here is caramelized and well seasoned. If fresh peaches are not readily available, use whatever fresh fruit is best at the time of year—apples, cherries, or oranges. Serve with wild rice.

- 4 domestic ducklings, 4 to 5 pounds each
- 4 to 6 tablespoons Creole Meat Seasoning (page 190)

Rich Duck Stock

(MAKES 1½ QUARTS)

- Carcasses from 4 ducklings
- 3 quarts water
- 1 cup coarsely chopped carrots
- 1 cup coarsely chopped onions
- 1 cup coarsely chopped celery
- ½ teaspoon thyme
- ½ teaspoon basil
- 2 bay leaves
- ½ cup tomato purée
- ½ cup crushed fresh tomatoes
- 1 clove of garlic, split
- ⅛ teaspoon nutmeg
- ⅛ teaspoon ginger

- 5 pounds very ripe fresh peaches

Caramel

- 1 cup sugar
- ¼ cup freshly squeezed orange juice
- ¼ cup fresh peach juice (see step 6)
- Juice of ½ lemon

Sauce

- 1 tablespoon vanilla extract
- ¾ teaspoon cinnamon
- ¼ teaspoon nutmeg
- ⅛ teaspoon ginger
- ¼ teaspoon oregano
- ⅛ teaspoon basil
- ¼ teaspoon thyme
- ½ cup peach juice (see step 6)
- 6 tablespoons cornstarch
- ⅓ cup ice water
- 32 slices fresh peaches, blanched
- ¼ cup peach brandy

1 ■ Roast ducklings in advance. Remove liver, gizzard, and neck from inside of each duckling. Rub ducklings inside and out with a liberal amount of meat seasoning.

2 ■ Preheat oven to 325°.

3 ■ Put ducklings on roasting rack and roast for 2 hours, or until juices run clear when thigh is pricked deeply with a fork.

4 ■ When ducklings are cooked, split them and carefully remove all bones, saving them for the stock. Put halved ducklings with skin on in refrigerator.

5 ■ *To make the stock:* Put stock ingredients in a large pot and bring to a boil. Reduce heat and simmer for 4 hours, then strain, mashing the bones to get all the flavor. Cook strained liquid until reduced to 1½ quarts. Set aside.

6 ■ Cut an X into base of each peach. Blanch in boiling water for 4 or 5 minutes. Remove peaches from water. Cool and peel. Cut cooked peaches into approximately 32 slices and save peach juice. You should have about ¾ cup juice for use in caramel and sauce.

7 ■ *To make the caramel:* Put ingredients in a heavy skillet and cook over medium heat, stirring occasionally, until the center of the mixture begins to turn brown. When caramel is the color of weak coffee, remove skillet from heat, but continue to stir for about 3 minutes, or until caramel is slightly cooled. Set aside.

8 ■ *To make the sauce:* Pour the stock into a large heavy saucepan. Bring to a quick boil, then whisk in the caramel and blend well. Add vanilla extract, cinnamon, nutmeg, ginger, oregano, basil, thyme, and peach juice. Mix well and bring to a boil. Combine cornstarch and ice water and stir into boiling stock mixture. Bring sauce back to a boil, reduce to a simmer, and, just before serving, drop peach slices into the sauce and stir in brandy.

9 ■ *To serve:* Preheat oven to 400°. Reheat ducklings in the oven until skin is crisp, about 10 minutes. Put half a duckling on each warmed plate and ladle ⅓ cup sauce and 4 peach slices over each half.

Roast Quail with Dirty Rice

SERVES 3

Small, tender baby quail are an elegant breakfast or brunch dish. Be careful not to burn the roux when making the sauce, which contains the Creole "Holy Trinity" of chopped onions, celery, and green bell pepper as well as garlic, thyme, and Creole meat seasoning. Accompany with a hearty red wine such as a Pommard or a Nuits St. Georges.

Dirty Rice

(MAKES 4 CUPS)

- 3¾ cups Chicken Stock (page 192)
- 1½ cups raw rice
- 1 tablespoon plus 5 teaspoons Creole Meat Seasoning (page 190)
- 8 tablespoons (1 stick) unsalted butter
- ½ cup coarsely ground chicken livers
- ½ cup coarsely ground chicken gizzards
- ½ cup coarsely ground pork
- ¾ cup chopped onions
- ½ cup chopped celery
- ½ cup chopped green bell pepper
- ½ cup chopped green onion tops
- 2 tablespoons minced garlic

- 8 tablespoons (1 stick) unsalted butter
- ¾ cup chopped onions
- ¾ cup chopped celery
- ¾ cup chopped green bell pepper
- 1 teaspoon salt
- ½ teaspoon freshly ground black pepper
- 1 clove of garlic, minced
- ½ teaspoon thyme
- 6 quail (2 per person, 6 ounces each)
- Creole Meat Seasoning (page 190)

Quail Sauce

- 3 tablespoons oil
- 3 tablespoons all-purpose flour
- 1 tablespoon unsalted butter
- 3 tablespoons grated onions
- 2 cups double-strength Chicken Stock (page 192)
- 2 tablespoons Burgundy
- 1 teaspoon salt
- ½ teaspoon freshly ground black pepper
- ½ teaspoon dried thyme
- 1 clove of garlic, minced

Garnish

- 6 fresh artichoke hearts poached in 1 cup chicken stock (page 192)

1 *To make dirty rice:* Bring 2¼ cups chicken stock to a boil in a 4-quart saucepan. Add the rice and Creole meat seasoning. Cover saucepan tightly and cook over low heat until rice has absorbed all the stock, 20 to 25 minutes.

2 Meanwhile, melt butter in another 4-quart saucepan and sauté ground livers, gizzards, and pork until lightly browned. Add onions, celery, green bell pepper, green onions, and garlic and cook for 20 minutes on medium heat.

3 Add the remaining stock and boil over medium high heat for 15 minutes.

4 Stir in 4 cups of cooked rice and cook until all stock is absorbed, about 10 to 15 minutes longer. Set aside.

5 To prepare the quail: Preheat oven to 350°.

6 Melt butter in a large skillet and sauté onions, celery, and green bell pepper along with salt, pepper, garlic, and thyme until vegetables are tender. Empty mixture into an 11x7x2-inch baking pan.

7 Season quail inside and out with meat seasoning and stuff with dirty rice. Put quail on bed of vegetables, cover with aluminum foil, and bake for 35 minutes. Remove foil, raise oven temperature to 375°, and roast for another 15 minutes.

8 *To make the sauce:* While quail are roasting, heat oil and flour in a small saucepan, blending with a wire whisk. Whisk the roux over medium heat until it is blond and bubbling. Set aside.

9 Melt butter in a heavy skillet and sauté onion for 2 minutes. Add stock and mix well. Stir in roux until all ingredients are well blended. Add wine and seasonings and stir until sauce is smooth. Set aside.

10 *To prepare the garnish:* Just before serving, thinly slice the artichoke hearts and poach them in stock for 3 minutes. Drain.

Roast Goose with Red Cabbage and Apples

SERVES 8

We serve roast goose at Commander's Palace every Thanksgiving to give people an alternative to turkey. We use a traditional recipe, adding New Orleans seasonings, and serve the goose with red cabbage and apples, an old German accompaniment. Alternatively, you might serve it with Yams Richard (page 139) and Cranberry Relish (page 139).

- 1 young goose, about 11 to 12 pounds, ready to cook
- Salt and freshly ground black pepper
- 5 sage leaves, chopped
- 1 sprig rosemary
- 6 cups Chicken Stock (page 192)
- 1 cup chopped onions
- ½ teaspoon black peppercorns
- 8 tablespoons (1 stick) unsalted butter, melted

Red Cabbage and Apples

- 2 medium heads red cabbage, shredded
- 1 cup sliced apple
- 1 cup Burgundy
- Juice of 1 lemon
- 1 teaspoon sugar
- 1 large onion, thinly sliced
- 1 apple, finely diced
- Salt and freshly ground black pepper

- 2 tablespoons all-purpose flour
- 2 cups red Burgundy

1 ■ Rinse and drain the goose. Cover with cold water and let stand for 15 minutes. Drain and pat dry inside and out. Remove excess fat from cavity and reserve for the cabbage.

2 ■ Preheat oven to 325°.

3 ■ Rub outside with salt and pepper. Sprinkle salt, pepper, sage, and rosemary in the cavity. Put breast up on rack in roasting pan. Add 4 cups stock, onions, and peppercorns. Basting frequently with butter, cook in the oven until the stock in roasting pan evaporates. Roast until tender, a total of about 2 hours. Goose is cooked when juices run clear from thigh when pricked deeply with a fork.

4 ■ *To prepare the cabbage and apples:* While the goose is cooking, combine cabbage, apples, wine, lemon juice, and sugar. Marinate 1 hour, tossing occasionally.

5 ■ Put reserved goose fat in a skillet and cook over low heat until all the liquid fat is rendered out. Pour 3 tablespoons of the fat into a heavy saucepan or kettle. Add cabbage and apple and a dash each of salt and pepper. Cover and braise over medium heat until cabbage and apple are tender, 20 to 30 minutes.

6 Remove goose from roasting pan. Remove all the meat from the goose and keep warm.

7 Put the bones in the roasting pan, sprinkle with flour, and sauté for a few minutes. Add remaining 2 cups chicken stock and the wine and cook a few minutes longer, stirring constantly. Strain.

8 *To serve:* Pour sauce over slices of goose and serve with cabbage and apples.

Grilled Louisiana Pigeon

SERVES 6

Make this dish only with fresh pigeons, which can be deboned by the butcher if this job seems too time-consuming. Marinated in Creole mustard, they have a wonderful piquant flavor. We served these pigeons at our Commander's 100th Anniversary Dinner, accompanied by a wonderful, full-bodied Duckhorn Merlot 1981. Delicious!

- 6 fresh pigeons, boned (reserve the bones)
- 2 teaspoons Creole Meat Seasoning (page 190)
- 2 tablespoons Creole or Dijon mustard
- ½ pound (2 sticks) unsalted butter
- 1 stalk celery, diced
- 1 medium onion, diced
- 2 sprigs fresh rosemary
- 1 bay leaf
- 15 whole black peppercorns
- 4 cups Chicken Stock (page 192)
- ½ cup red wine

1 Rub pigeons with seasoning and mustard and let sit at room temperature for about 1 hour.

2 Preheat oven to 350°.

3 Heat a heavy ovenproof skillet and melt 4 tablespoons (½ stick) butter. Brown pigeons on all sides, then transfer to oven for 12 minutes.

4 In an iron skillet heat another 4 tablespoons butter. Add pigeon bones and cook over high heat for about 10 minutes. Reduce heat to moderate and add celery, onion, rosemary, bay leaf, and peppercorns and cook for 10 minutes longer. Add stock and wine and simmer for about 30 minutes.

5 Strain stock into a saucepan and cook over high heat until reduced to 2 cups.

6 Remove pigeons from skillet in which they were cooked, pour the sauce into the skillet, and cook while stirring in all the juices and pigeon glaze from the pan. Remove from heat and stir in remaining butter, bit by bit. Serve over the pigeons.

Roast Turkey with Oyster Dressing and Giblet Mushroom Sauce

SERVES 8 TO 10

Turkey at Commander's is very highly seasoned with our Creole meat seasoning. Yams Richard and cranberry-orange relish are easy-to-prepare accompaniments.

- 1 fresh turkey, about 18 pounds, ready to cook
- Creole Meat Seasoning (page 190)

Oyster Dressing

- ¼ plus ⅛ pound (1½ sticks) unsalted butter
- 4 cups diced onions
- 2½ cups diced celery
- 1½ cups diced green bell pepper
- 4 bay leaves
- 4½ dozen oysters, chopped (reserve liquor) (see footnote page 23)
- 1½ teaspoons minced garlic
- 9 cups fresh bread crumbs
- 3 cups dry bread crumbs
- 1½ teaspoons salt
- 3 tablespoons Creole Seafood Seasoning (page 190)

Giblet Mushroom Gravy

- 2 quarts strong Chicken Stock (page 192)
- 5 tablespoons unsalted butter
- ⅓ cup all-purpose flour
- 1 cup chopped onions
- 1 cup chopped green bell pepper
- 2½ cups sliced fresh mushrooms
- ½ cup Burgundy

1 ▪ Set aside neck and giblets and rub turkey inside and out with meat seasoning or seasoning of your choice.

2 ▪ *To make oyster dressing:* Melt butter in a heavy skillet and sauté onions, celery, green bell pepper, and bay leaves until wilted. Add oysters and garlic and cook for 10 minutes.

3 ▪ Moisten fresh bread crumbs with 4 cups oyster liquor. Add moistened bread crumbs and dry bread crumbs to the vegetable-oyster mixture and mix lightly. Add salt and seafood seasoning and cook for 10 minutes. Preheat oven to 300°.

4 ▪ Turn turkey breast down and fill neck cavity loosely with stuffing. Pull neck skin over stuffing and secure to back of turkey with skewers. Turn turkey breast side up, fold wing tips under, and fill cavity lightly with remaining stuffing. Tie legs together over cavity opening or, if your turkey has a metal clamp, return it to its original position, holding the legs in place. Put turkey on rack in open roasting pan, breast up, and roast in the preheated oven for about 8 hours, or until juice that runs from the thigh when pierced deeply with a fork is clear.

5 *To make gravy:* Cook neck and giblets in stock for 2 to 3 hours, or until they are very tender and the stock is reduced to about 5 cups. Chop giblets and tender meat from the neck and set aside separately from the stock.

6 Melt butter in a small skillet. Add flour and whisk over medium heat until roux is smooth and golden. Stir it into the stock. Add onions and green bell pepper and simmer for 25 to 30 minutes. Strain stock, return to heat, and add giblets and neck meat, mushrooms, and wine. Cook 5 minutes longer before serving.

7 Transfer turkey to a warmed serving platter and carve. Serve some sliced white and dark meat to each person, along with a spoonful of stuffing and a generous serving of gravy.

Note: Do not stuff turkey with the warm dressing until just before roasting. If you want to stuff turkey in advance, make the stuffing ahead of time, let cool, then chill thoroughly before using to stuff the bird.

Yams Richard

SERVES 4

- 4 sweet potatoes
- ¼ cup coarsely chopped pecans
- 2 tablespoons brown sugar
- ¼ pound (1 stick) unsalted butter
- Pinch of ground cinnamon
- Miniature marshmallows

1 Bake sweet potatoes until soft. Peel them and cut into fourths, place in bowl, add remaining ingredients, except marshmallows, and mix with electric beater while still warm, which helps the butter to melt and blend. Raise the beaters and remove any "strings" in the sweet potatoes.

2 When well mixed and smooth, spoon into buttered casserole dish. Sprinkle marshmallows on top and bake in 350° oven until marshmallows are golden.

Cranberry Relish for Turkey or Goose

SERVES 8

- 1 pound cranberries
- 2 oranges, peeled
- 1 cup sugar
- 1 ounce rum
- 1 ounce Grand Marnier

Put all ingredients in container of blender or food processor and mince finely. Refrigerate overnight.

Beef and Veal

In the nineteenth century, before modern transportation, Creole cooks did not use very much beef or veal, because it was hard to come by; Creole cuisine was mainly based on everything that swam or waddled in native waters. Cooks had to learn to make imaginative and economical use of what little beef or veal they had, and developed beef dishes in the style of country or provincial "pot cooking"—stews like boeuf en daube or smothered dishes like grillades—in which the meats were cooked for hours to tenderize them. Recipes were handed down by French, Spanish, and Italian ancestors, then modified and improved to adapt to the Creole style of cooking.

Today, however, there is excellent quality beef and milk-fed baby veal available in this country, so at Commander's we have been doing more with beef dishes, "Creolizing" them with our special seasonings and the "Holy Trinity" of Creole vegetables—onions, celery, and bell pepper—and combining them with interesting and unusual flourless sauces. We have shortened the cooking time to bring out the full flavor of the meat, and prepare almost everything rare unless specifically requested not to. Frying has been virtually replaced by quick sautéing. This means that many of these beef and veal dishes are simple and quick to make for the home chef.

The new Haute Creole beef and veal dishes are distinctive because of their intense New Orleans seasonings, and the unique combinations of sauces that so much depend on the quality of the stocks. For the most part we avoid the old-fashioned flour-based roux to thicken our sauces, using instead reductions of natural juices to create intense and lasting flavors.

We have updated many of the classic beef and veal dishes with new Haute Creole methods. For instance, panéed veal now uses only superior-quality milk-fed

veal and is sautéed for mere minutes (instead of fried) and served with fresh homemade fettuccine. We have modified the famous New Orleans grillades, improving the quality of the ingredients, shortening the cooking time, and replacing the heavy Creole sauce with a new light tomato sauce. Our veal dishes range from the plain to the fancy: from veal Kottwitz, a simple sauté with fresh mushrooms and artichokes, to tenderloin of veal citron stuffed with pâté de foie gras. Another good example of Haute Creole is veal or beef tenderloin Tchoupitoulas, quickly sautéed and served with a rich sauce of port wine, demi-glace, and currant jelly, reduced to intensify and deepen the flavor.

Updated beef classics include filet mignon Stanley and tournedos provençale, with a colorful medley of fresh diced vegetables sautéed briefly. We have also tried to adapt simple country Cajun recipes, like filet mignon debris, which has an interesting smoky flavor.

The Haute Creole style of cooking demands great care in selecting the best possible raw materials, and cooking methods are chosen purposefully to bring out the full flavor and textures of these fresh ingredients.

Chapter opening illustration: *The formal dining rooms on the first floor of Commander's Palace, with mahogany wood details and antique chandeliers, are intimate in scale and create the feeling of dining in someone's private home.*

Tournedos Provençale

SERVES 4

Of Mediterranean inspiration, tournedos provençale is an unusual combination of sautéed filet mignon, lightly garlicked tomato, and lots of fresh diced vegetables. If you chop the vegetables ahead, this dish takes just minutes to prepare. You must use only fresh vine-ripened tomatoes; if you can't find any, do not make this dish. Garnish with briefly sautéed crisp vegetables. Serve with a full-bodied red wine.

- 4 filets mignons, about 6 ounces each
- ¼ teaspoon Creole Meat Seasoning (page 190)
- 8 tablespoons (1 stick) unsalted butter
- 1 cup coarsely chopped onions
- 1 cup peeled, seeded, diced fresh tomatoes
- 6 large mushrooms, quartered
- 4 cloves of garlic, minced
- ¼ cup minced parsley
- 2 teaspoons cracked black pepper

1 ■ Dust filets with meat seasoning.

2 ■ Heat 3 tablespoons butter in a sauté pan. When butter foams, add filets and sauté to doneness desired, about 2 to 3 minutes on each side. Remove and set aside on a warm platter.

3 ■ To butter and juices remaining in pan add onions, tomatoes, mushrooms, garlic, and parsley. Stir gently and cook until onions are almost transparent. Add pepper and remaining butter. Remove from heat and stir gently with a wooden spoon until butter is melted and sauce has a creamy look.

4 ■ Spoon sauce over the filets and serve immediately.

Tournedos Coliseum

SERVES 4

An old favorite at Commander's Palace; two small filets mignons are served, one covered with a dark marchand de vins sauce, the other with a light béarnaise. Serve with fresh seasonal vegetables, such as broccoli, and a fine Bordeaux or California Cabernet Sauvignon.

8 tournedos of beef, 3 to 4 ounces each
Creole Meat Seasoning (page 190)
8 tablespoons Marchand de Vins Sauce (page 198)
8 tablespoons Béarnaise Sauce (page 196)

1 Season meat well and broil or sauté to desired degree of doneness.

2 Put 2 tournedos side by side on each well-heated plate. Cover one with marchand de vins sauce and the other with béarnaise. Serve immediately.

Filet Mignon Stanley

SERVES 6

An unusual combination of beef, Creole seasonings, creamed horseradish, and sautéed curried bananas, this is a classic whose success has been proven by the test of time. It must be tasted! Use only fresh horseradish.

2 cups heavy cream
Salt and freshly ground white pepper
3 tablespoons shredded fresh horseradish (*not* prepared)
6 filets mignons, 6 to 8 ounces each
2 teaspoons Creole Meat Seasoning (page 190)
10 tablespoons butter
6 bananas
2 teaspoons curry powder

1 Preheat oven to 350°.

2 Bring cream to a boil in a heavy saucepan over medium-high heat and boil rapidly until reduced to one third its original quantity, or about ⅔ cup. Add a pinch each of salt and pepper and stir in horseradish. Set aside and keep warm.

3 Sprinkle filets with Creole seasoning and sauté in 6 tablespoons butter in a hot iron skillet to doneness desired, 2 to 3 minutes on each side.

4 While filets are cooking, melt remaining butter in a 9x12-inch baking pan. Peel bananas, cut lengthwise, and arrange in the pan in the melted butter. Turn to coat bananas on both sides, sprinkle with curry powder, and bake until slightly soft, about 5 minutes.

5 *To serve:* Put a heaping tablespoon of horseradish sauce on each plate, place a filet on top, and garnish with 2 banana halves.

Filet Mignon Adelaide

SERVES 4

This is an extremely elegant beef dish named after our sister Adelaide, who happened not to be around to defend herself when we were trying to name it. The regal presentation of filet mignon in a pool of demi-glace, crowned with fresh artichoke bottoms stuffed with sweetbreads or veal, tomatoes, and mushrooms, topped with a rich béarnaise, offers an occasion to serve your best Bordeaux.

- 4 filets mignons, 6 to 8 ounces each
- 4 teaspoons Creole Meat Seasoning (page 190)

Forcemeat Stuffing

- ½ pound ground veal or sweetbreads
- 1 medium onion, finely chopped
- 8 tablespoons (1 stick) unsalted butter
- ½ pound fresh mushrooms, finely chopped
- 3 tomatoes, peeled and finely chopped
- Salt and freshly ground pepper to taste
- ¼ cup bread crumbs (optional)

- 4 cooked fresh artichoke bottoms
- 1 cup Demi-glace (page 193), heated
- 1 cup Béarnaise Sauce (page 196), heated

Garnish

- Watercress

1 Sprinkle meat with seasoning and broil or sauté to the desired degree of doneness. Set aside and keep warm, with artichoke bottoms.

2 *To make stuffing:* Sauté meat and onion in butter until onion is transparent and meat is brown. Add mushrooms, tomatoes, and salt and pepper and simmer for 10 to 15 minutes. If mixture is too wet, add bread crumbs to sop up the excess. Correct seasoning to taste. Remove from heat and refrigerate.

3 When stuffing is cold and firm, stuff each artichoke bottom with a small mound of it. Smooth off the top.

4 *To serve:* Put ¼ cup warm demi-glace on each well-heated plate and put a filet mignon on top. Top with an artichoke bottom and béarnaise sauce. Garnish with watercress.

Filet Mignon Debris

SERVES 8

Based on the experienced cook's knowledge that what's left in the pan after roasting—bones and bits of caramelized vegetables—is always the best part, we developed this unusual entree. The bones and vegetables are intentionally burned "to a blue smoke," and the dish has a special smoky flavor, which some people love but others may find an acquired taste.

- 3 beef bones, 6 inches long, cut into 1-inch pieces
- 1 cup diced celery
- 4 cups diced onions
- 2½ cups diced green bell pepper
- 1 cup chopped green onions
- 5 teaspoons Creole Meat Seasoning (page 190)
- 2½ cups Brown Sauce (page 193)
- 2½ cups Beef Stock (page 192)
- 1½ cups ground steak trimmings with fat, preferably from sirloin
- ¼ cup red wine
- 2½ teaspoons brandy
- 8 filets mignons, 6 to 8 ounces each

1 ■ Preheat oven to 500°.

2 ■ Put bones, celery, onions, green bell pepper, and green onions in a large roasting pan. Sprinkle with 3 teaspoons meat seasoning. Stirring occasionally, roast until all ingredients are caramelized and burned black, about 2 hours.

3 ■ Remove from oven and add brown sauce and stock. Mix well with the charred debris. Reduce oven temperature to 350° and roast for 1 hour longer.

4 ■ Scatter ground beef trimmings in bottom of a small roasting pan and cook in the oven along with the debris until meat is very dry and crusty.

5 ■ Remove the debris from oven and strain the sauce in the pan through a very fine strainer into a saucepan. Bring to a boil over high heat, stirring constantly. Stir in steak trimmings and return to a boil. Add wine and brandy and set sauce aside. Keep warm. Makes 2 cups sauce.

6 ■ Season the filets with remaining meat seasoning and broil or sauté in hot butter to desired degree of doneness.

7 ■ *To serve:* Put a filet on each warmed plate and ladle ¼ cup sauce on top.

■ ***Note:*** This recipe will not work unless the bones are burned black. It is not for timid cooks!

Sliced Roast Tenderloin of Beef with Anchovy Butter

SERVES 6 TO 8

This is the easiest beef dish in the world, but a great favorite with us. The simplicity of the dish demands perfection: the best cut of meat and a great bottle of wine.

1 whole tenderloin of beef, nicely trimmed, 3½ to 4 pounds

2 tablespoons Creole Meat Seasoning (page 190)

Anchovy Butter

½ pound (2 sticks) unsalted butter

10 anchovy fillets

1 tablespoon minced parsley

1 ■ Preheat oven to 425°.

2 ■ Season meat well, put in shallow roasting pan, and roast for 25 minutes, or until done to your taste.

3 ■ Melt butter in a skillet until very pale beige in color. Add anchovies and parsley and stir gently.

4 ■ *To serve:* Slice tenderloin, cover with anchovy butter, and serve immediately.

Steak Diane with New Potatoes and Parsley Butter

SERVES 4

There are many other versions of Steak Diane, but this is the Brennan family favorite, one of the first dishes our children learned to cook. We like it very simple: Sauté the slices of seasoned tenderloin in butter, deglaze the pan with Worcestershire sauce and steak sauce, add chopped parsley, and spoon the sauce over the beef. Garnish with watercress and serve with boiled new potatoes with parsley butter.

Parsley Butter

- 8 tablespoons (1 stick) unsalted butter, softened
- 1 tablespoon finely chopped parsley

- 12 slices beef tenderloin, each about 2½ ounces
- 2 teaspoons Creole Meat Seasoning (page 190)
- 8 tablespoons (1 stick) unsalted butter
- 1 tablespoon Worcestershire sauce
- 1 tablespoon A-1 steak sauce
- ½ cup finely chopped parsley
- 1½ pounds new potatoes, boiled

Garnish

Watercress

1 ■ *To make parsley butter:* Mash parsley into butter and scrape into a small crock. Refrigerate until ready to use.

2 ■ Season meat with meat seasoning.

3 ■ Melt butter in a hot iron skillet and quickly sauté tenderloins to desired degree of doneness. Remove meat to a warm serving platter and keep warm.

3 ■ Add Worcestershire sauce and steak sauce to butter remaining in skillet and cook, stirring in all bits of meat glaze from bottom and sides of pan. Add parsley.

4 ■ When the sauce is reduced slightly, pour it over the beef and garnish with watercress. Serve with boiled new potatoes and parsley butter.

Beef Tenderloin with Tchoupitoulas Sauce

SERVES 4

Named after an old Louisiana Indian tribe and a well-known New Orleans Street, this new beef dish is light and very elegant. If you have the demi-glace on hand, it can be prepared in minutes. You can also substitute medallions of veal, scallopini, or double veal chops. Serve with a full-bodied California Cabernet Sauvignon.

- ¼ pound (1 stick) unsalted butter, softened
- 8 scallops of beef tenderloin, 2½ ounces each
- 1 teaspoon Creole Meat Seasoning (page 190)
- ½ cup Demi-glace (page 193)
- 2 teaspoons currant jelly
- ¼ cup port

1 ■ Heat an iron skillet until very hot. Add half the butter. Season meat with meat seasoning and sauté quickly on both sides, turning only once, until cooked to desired degree of doneness. Remove to warm platter and keep warm.

2 ■ To butter and juices remaining in skillet add the demi-glace, jelly, and port. Cook, stirring in all the bits of glaze from bottom and sides of pan, until sauce is reduced to half its original quantity. Add remaining butter and swirl pan over heat until butter is just melted and the sauce has a translucent glaze. Do not let it boil.

3 ■ Pour sauce over the beef and serve immediately.

Panéed Veal and Fettuccine

SERVES 6

This is an old New Orleans breaded veal dish that we have lightened and brought up to Haute Creole by improving the quality of the raw materials. Use only superior-quality milk-fed baby veal, homemade fettuccine, and freshly grated Parmesan and Romano cheeses. Panéed veal used to be more of a peasant-style dish, but now if Queen Elizabeth wanted to come to dinner, it would be a dish worthy of Her Majesty.

- 6 thin slices white veal, 3 to 4 ounces each
- Salt, freshly ground black pepper, and cayenne pepper to taste
- 3 whole eggs
- ½ cup freshly grated Parmesan cheese
- 2½ cups finely ground fresh white bread crumbs
- ½ cup Clarified Butter (page 195)

- ½ pound fettuccine noodles
- 1 tablespoon olive oil

Cheese Sauce

- 8 tablespoons (1 stick) unsalted butter
- 1 cup freshly grated Parmesan cheese
- 1 cup freshly grated Romano cheese
- 1 pint (2 cups) heavy cream
- Dash of cayenne pepper

1 Season veal with salt, black pepper, and cayenne pepper. Beat eggs until light and stir in cheese. Dip veal in egg mixture, then coat evenly with bread crumbs. Sauté quickly in clarified butter until lightly browned on both sides, turning once. Set aside and keep warm.

2 Cook fettuccine according to directions on package. Drain and rinse in cold water. Pour oil over the noodles and toss lightly. Set aside.

3 *To make cheese sauce:* Melt butter in a 2-quart saucepan over low heat. Add Parmesan and Romano cheese and stir constantly over low heat until cheese melts. Do not let the sauce get too hot. Whisk the cream into the sauce. Add cayenne pepper. Set over hot water to keep warm until ready to serve.

4 *To serve:* Drop forkfuls of fettuccine into boiling water to reheat, twist into a knot, and put on warm serving plates. Ladle 3 tablespoons of sauce over each serving of noodles and put a slice of veal on the side. Serve immediately.

Note: The combination of freshly grated Romano and Parmesan melts more thoroughly than just Parmesan.

Veal Kottwitz

SERVES 4

This dish is based on a classic Italian combination of veal, artichokes, and mushrooms. We named it veal Kottwitz after a very good customer who loved it. It's a simple dish that can be made in minutes.

- 8 veal tenderloins or cutlets, about 2½ ounces each
- Creole Meat Seasoning (page 190)
- All-purpose flour
- 11 tablespoons (1 stick plus 3 tablespoons) unsalted butter
- 4 cooked artichoke bottoms, sliced
- 6 medium mushrooms, quartered
- 2 cloves of garlic, minced
- 1 cup minced green onions
- 4 ounces Chablis or other dry white wine
- Juice of ½ lemon
- ¼ teaspoon cayenne pepper

1 ■ Season veal with meat seasoning and dust lightly with flour.

2 ■ Melt 3 tablespoons butter in a large sauté pan. When bubbling, add veal and sauté until golden brown on both sides. Remove meat to warm platter and keep warm.

3 ■ To the warm butter in pan add artichoke bottoms, mushrooms, garlic, green onions, wine, and lemon juice. Simmer, uncovered, until liquid is reduced by a third. Add remaining butter and cayenne pepper and stir gently over low heat until butter is just melted and sauce is creamy. Pour over veal and serve immediately.

Veal Marcelle

SERVES 4

Named after a young woman who used to work at Commander's and recently opened her own restaurant in Broussard, Louisiana, in the middle of Cajun country, veal Marcelle is a Creole version of veal Oscar. The veal is spiced with our special Creole meat seasoning, briefly sautéed, and topped with a marvelous mixture of fresh lump crab meat, green onions, shallots, Worcestershire sauce, and hollandaise sauce. In season, asparagus makes a perfect accompaniment.

- 8 veal cutlets, 3 ounces each
- Creole Meat Seasoning (page 190)
- All-purpose flour for dredging
- 3 tablespoons unsalted butter
- ½ cup finely sliced green onions
- 2 medium shallots, finely chopped
- 1 cup fresh lump crab meat, shells carefully removed
- 2 teaspoons Worcestershire sauce
- 1 cup Hollandaise Sauce (page 199)

Garnish

Watercress

1 Pound cutlets ¼ inch thick between two pieces of parchment or waxed paper. Season with meat seasoning and dredge lightly in flour.

2 Heat butter in a sauté pan. When it is bubbling, add veal and sauté until golden brown on both sides, turning once. Remove meat and keep warm. To the hot butter remaining in pan add green onions, shallots, crab meat, and Worcestershire sauce. Cook, stirring, for 1 minute.

3 *To serve:* Arrange meat on a warm serving plate. Ladle the sauce in sauté pan over the meat and top with hollandaise. Garnish with watercress and serve immediately.

Veal Calvados

SERVES 4

A recipe of Swiss inspiration popular in New Orleans in the nineteenth century, veal Calvados is a unique combination of veal, apple, and onions in an apple brandy–wine sauce. In Switzerland it is served with apple beignets. A slightly spicy German Riesling would be the perfect wine to bring out the fresh-apple taste.

- 8 veal tenderloins or cutlets about ½ inch thick (2½ ounces each)
- 2 teaspoons Creole Meat Seasoning (page 190)
- All-purpose flour
- 3 tablespoons unsalted butter
- 8 apple rings, ¼ inch thick
- ½ cup diced peeled apple
- 1 cup diced onions
- ¼ cup coarsely chopped shallots
- 2 ounces Chablis
- 3 ounces Calvados (apple brandy)
- 10 tablespoons heavy cream
- 3 ounces Demi-glace (page 193)
- Freshly ground black pepper to taste

Garnish

- Watercress
- Cooked fresh asparagus

1 ■ Sprinkle veal with meat seasoning, then dredge lightly in flour. Heat butter in a sauté pan; when bubbling, add veal and sauté until lightly brown on both sides, turning once. Add apple rings to butter in pan and fry for about 1 minute on each side. Apple rings should remain crisp. Remove rings.

2 ■ Add to pan the diced apple, onions, shallots, Chablis, and Calvados. Stir gently over low heat. Remove veal and keep warm.

3 ■ Whisk cream and demi-glace into sauce in pan and bring to a simmer, whisking constantly. Return veal to pan and cook over low heat, uncovered, until tender, about 10 minutes. Do *not* put apple rings in pan.

4 ■ *To serve:* Arrange veal on top of apple slices and keep warm. Reduce sauce to the consistency of a thin cream sauce. Add a pinch of black pepper. Spoon sauce over veal and garnish platter with watercress and asparagus.

Veal Grillades

SERVES 10

An updated version of the classic Southern veal grillades; we have improved the quality of the ingredients and lightened it in the style of the new Haute Creole. In the old version, an inexpensive cut of veal was cooked for a long time and served with a heavy Creole sauce. In Commander's new version we use the best quality and best cut of veal, medallions or the fillet, and a very light Creole sauce. The traditional accompaniment is buttered grits to soak up the delicious sauce, but you can use rice.

- 20 medallions of veal, about 2 ounces each
- 1 teaspoon Creole Meat Seasoning (page 190)
- 1 cup all-purpose flour
- 4 tablespoons Clarified Butter (page 195)
- 2 tablespoons coarsely chopped green onions
- 1½ cups Creole Sauce (page 197)
- Crushed black pepper
- ¼ cup Chicken Stock (page 192) (optional)

1 ■ Pound veal between two pieces of parchment or waxed paper until very thin and trim into 2- or 3-inch squares. Combine meat seasoning and flour and dredge meat in seasoned flour. In a Dutch oven or large skillet, sauté the meat in a small amount of clarified butter, adding more if needed, until golden brown on both sides. Remove meat and set aside. Keep warm.

2 ■ To the Dutch oven or skillet add green onions and Creole sauce. Cook, stirring in all the flour sticking to bottom of the pan. It will thicken the sauce. Add the black pepper, about 2 pinches per serving, or to taste. If the sauce is too thick, stir in stock.

3 ■ Return meat to sauce and simmer on low heat for about 5 minutes, or until veal is tender. Serve over cooked rice or plain buttered grits.

Veal Roast with Oyster Dressing

SERVES 6

A hearty wintertime dish, roast of veal is an excellent party dish and can be prepared ahead. Serve with winter vegetables like sweet potatoes or squash.

- 1 boneless veal roast, about 3 pounds, bones and trimmings reserved
- 2 quarts water
- 1 tablespoon oil
- Salt and freshly ground black pepper
- 3 medium onions, chopped
- 3 stalks celery, chopped
- 6 to 8 cloves of garlic, minced
- 2 medium green bell peppers, chopped
- 2 bay leaves
- 1 cup Burgundy

Oyster Dressing

- ½ pound (2 sticks) unsalted butter
- 1 onion, coarsely chopped
- 1 heart of celery, coarsely chopped
- 1 medium green bell pepper, coarsely chopped
- 3 cloves of garlic, minced
- 3 bay leaves
- 1 teaspoon dried thyme
- 1 pint freshly shucked oysters with oyster liquor
- 1 tablespoon Worcestershire sauce
- 1 tablespoon Louisiana Red Hot Sauce
- About 4 cups dry bread crumbs or cubes

1 ■ Prepare a stock of the veal bones and trimmings and water. Simmer until liquid is reduced to 2 cups, about 2 hours. Set aside.

2 ■ *To make the dressing:* Heat butter and sauté onion, celery, green bell pepper, garlic, bay leaves, and thyme until tender. Add oysters and oyster liquor and stir gently. Add Worcestershire sauce and hot sauce. Bring to a boil. Remove from heat and stir in sufficient bread crumbs or cubes to make the desired consistency. Transfer dressing to an ovenproof casserole dish.

3 ■ Preheat oven to 350°.

4 ■ Brush roast with oil and sprinkle lightly with salt and pepper. Roast until brown, about 1½ hours. Add onions, celery, garlic, green bell pepper, and bay leaves and roast for 30 minutes longer, or until meat is done. Put casserole with dressing in same oven and bake for last 30 minutes.

5 ■ When roast is well cooked and vegetables are browned, add wine and 2 cups reduced stock. Return roast to oven and bake until liquid is reduced by half, being careful not to let the vegetables burn. This is the sauce to spoon over the roast. Remove roast and cool a little before slicing.

6 *To serve:* Spoon a portion of the dressing onto each warmed plate and put a slice of roast veal on top. Ladle some of the sauce over the meat and serve immediately.

Veal Lafayette

SERVES 4

Named after an area of the Garden District that used to be the City of Lafayette, incorporated in 1832, this is a very light and delicate crêpe dish. The thin crêpes, which can be made ahead, are filled with the luxurious Lafayette sauce; a mixture of ham, white veal, mushrooms, and Swiss cheese spiced with green onions and garlic, all bound with heavy cream and a roux. The crêpes give an elegant presentation and are versatile, for they can also be used as an appetizer or a lovely luncheon entree with a salad.

- 1 tablespoon unsalted butter
- 1 tablespoon all-purpose flour

Lafayette Sauce

- 1 tablespoon unsalted butter
- ½ cup finely diced ham
- ½ cup finely chopped white veal
- 1 cup sliced mushrooms
- ¼ cup minced green onions
- 1 clove of garlic, minced
- ½ teaspoon salt and freshly ground pepper
- ½ cup heavy cream
- 4 thin slices Swiss cheese, ½ ounce each

- 4 Crêpes (page 164)

1 Melt 1 tablespoon butter over medium heat. Add flour, blending with a wire whisk, and whisk constantly until the roux is blond and bubbling. Remove from heat and set aside.

2 Melt 1 tablespoon butter in a sauté pan. Add ham and veal and sauté lightly for a minute or so. Add mushrooms, green onions, garlic, and salt and pepper. Cook for a few minutes, stirring gently. Add cream. Let sauce come to a boil, add roux, and whisk continuously until sauce is hot and smooth. Reduce heat and simmer for 5 minutes.

3 *To serve:* Spoon some of the sauce onto each crêpe. Fold crêpe over and put 1 slice of cheese on top. Put in oven or under broiler until cheese is melted. Serve immediately.

Veal with Wild Mushrooms

SERVES 4

A luxurious and exotic dish that can be made with as many kinds of fresh wild mushrooms as you can find. This dish can live up to the most regal of clarets, so pull out all the stops.

- 8 veal cutlets, about 3 ounces each, well pounded
- Creole Meat Seasoning (page 190)
- 3 tablespoons unsalted butter
- 4 medium shallots, chopped
- 4 ounces fresh wild mushrooms (chanterelles or morels)
- 2 ounces cultivated mushrooms
- 1 ounce brandy
- ¼ cup red wine
- ¾ cup Demi-glace (page 193)
- ¼ cup heavy cream
- Salt and freshly ground black pepper

Garnish

- Watercress

1 ■ Season veal with meat seasoning and sauté in hot melted butter until lightly browned on both sides, turning once. Remove and keep warm.

2 ■ To butter remaining in pan add shallots and mushrooms and sauté for 1 minute. Add brandy, wine, demi-glace, and cream. Add salt and pepper if needed, and simmer for about 5 minutes.

3 ■ *To serve:* Arrange veal on warm serving plate, ladle sauce over veal, and garnish with watercress.

■ ***Note:*** Morels and chanterelles, wild mushrooms usually imported from Switzerland or France, are available either fresh or dried in specialty food shops or at Oriental greengrocers.

Tenderloin of Veal Citron with Pâté de Foie Gras

SERVES 6

A fabulous and impressive party dish, as you can tell by the luxurious ingredients, veal citron was created by Chef Brill in Berlin in the 1960s on the occasion of a state visit by President John F. Kennedy. The veal can be stuffed easily—first push a sharpening steel through the center of the tenderloin and then push the cold pâté through. Slice the meat vertically in rounds, put on a heated decorative platter, and ladle on top the strong, aromatic lemon-flavored sauce that gives the dish its name. It can be served with plain buttered fettuccine for contrast to the richness of the foie gras.

- 2 whole veal tenderloins, about 3 pounds total
- 6 ounces pâté de fois gras
- 1 teaspoon Creole Meat Seasoning (page 190)
- 8 tablespoons (1 stick) unsalted butter
- ¼ cup chopped shallots
- 2 teaspoons finely chopped tarragon
- ¼ cup finely chopped parsley
- Juice of 5 lemons
- 9 ounces (1 cup plus 2 tablespoons) dry white wine
- 1 pint (2 cups) heavy cream, whipped

1 Make a hole lengthwise in the veal tenderloins with a sharpening steel. Stuff the hole with foie gras. Sprinkle seasoning over the veal.

2 Preheat a large skillet and add butter. When butter is foaming hot, add veal and sauté for 10 minutes, turning so that it browns evenly on all sides. Remove meat from skillet.

3 To skillet add shallots, tarragon, parsley, lemon juice, and wine, and cook over moderate heat, stirring in all the nice bits of veal glaze from bottom and sides of skillet. Cook the sauce until reduced and slightly thickened. Gradually whisk in the whipped cream.

4 Slice meat and arrange on a warm platter. Top with sauce and serve immediately.

Desserts and Coffees

Even in this calorie-conscious era, the Southern sweet tooth survives. Creoles are famous for their sumptuous desserts. They can be elaborate and glamorous creations, such as flaming baked Alaska or poached pears in pistachio sauce, for the finale to an elegant dinner party, or soothing and simple home-style recipes, such as caramel cup custard or bread pudding.

The Commander's menu features a large selection of such Southern classics as bananas Foster, crêpes Suzette, and pecan pie. But it also includes such interesting new creations as homemade Creole cream cheese ice cream, with a rich taste that is both sweet and tart; our celebration dessert, a chocolate-covered bombe encasing vanilla ice cream and raspberry mousse; and bread pudding soufflé, a lighter version of the old favorite.

For home entertaining, a selection of several desserts set out on a specially decorated table (perhaps in another room) creates a festive, fun atmosphere for guests. Many desserts can be prepared in advance, making it all easy. At the end of a meal, a lavish display of desserts is an extravagant and welcome gesture.

With sweets, New Orleanians love to drink their own special coffee, either black (café noir), with milk (café au lait), or, as a special treat, flamed with spices and liqueurs. Creoles describe their coffee as:

Noir comme le Diable
Fort comme la Mort
Doux comme l'Amour
Et chaud comme l'Enfer.

This means they like their coffee black as the devil, strong as death, sweet as love, and hot as hell!

According to New Orleans folklore, the regular intake of café noir not only acts as a powerful stimulant but contributes to longevity and aids digestion. At one time, it was believed to prevent infectious disease.

The French Market is famous for its twenty-four-hour coffee stands, and a cup of steamy café au lait, traditionally served with freshly made, hot beignets (deep-fried doughnuts without holes, dusted with powdered sugar), is a favorite treat.

New Orleans coffee is made from a complex blend of coffees and ground roasted chicory; it is a potent beverage—aromatic, rich, smooth, with great body. The chicory makes the coffee stronger and thicker and adds a slightly bitter flavor. Even without chicory, New Orleans coffee is a powerful brew, from a much darker roast than you find elsewhere in the United States. We don't use espresso here because our regular chicory coffee is so strong.

The practice of combining chicory with coffee developed in France during the Napoleonic era, when a blockade against English shipping meant Europeans could not get the coffee they loved so. A barley drink was first substituted, but it had a bland flavor, so chicory, which has a full-bodied, pungent taste, was used to improve the barley drink. When the blockade ended with the fall of Napoleon, coffee reappeared. But the strong chicory flavor had become popular, and since chicory was less expensive than coffee, the frugal French continued to use it to stretch their coffee.

At Commander's we use a blend of Brazilian and Central American coffees, combined with 20 to 35 percent chicory. The exact amount varies among blenders and is a trade secret. Our chicory is roasted and ground in France.

French Market chicory-blend coffee in cans is becoming available in gourmet shops and fine food departments in many parts of the country.

Chapter opening illustration: *Flaming coffees and desserts are one of our specialties at Commander's. Here, the captain prepares café brûlot.*

Bananas Foster

SERVES 2

New Orleans is a banana-importing city and bananas are prepared in many ways for favorite desserts. This particularly rich and wicked dessert came about to honor a friend of our brother Owen's, Dick Foster, who during the fifties was serving as vice-chairman of the Vice Committee in charge of cleaning up the French Quarter. Bananas are sautéed in brown sugar and cinnamon, flambéed with banana liqueur and rum, and served over vanilla ice cream. As a variation, you can substitute banana ice cream or Creole Cream Cheese Ice Cream (page 177).

- 4 tablespoons (½ stick) unsalted butter
- 4 tablespoons brown sugar
- 2 ripe bananas, peeled and sliced lengthwise
- ¼ teaspoon cinnamon
- 2 tablespoons banana liqueur
- 3 ounces light or dark rum
- 1½ cups French Vanilla Ice Cream (page 172)

1 ■ Melt butter in a flat chafing dish or skillet. Add brown sugar and stir until sugar is melted. Add bananas and sauté until tender, about 3 minutes on each side. Sprinkle with cinnamon.

2 ■ Pour banana liqueur and rum over bananas, shake pan to distribute the liquid, and flame. Baste bananas with the flaming sauce until flames die out.

3 ■ Serve immediately over the ice cream.

Crêpes Suzette

SERVES 4

Crêpes Suzette is the most elegant of all crêpe desserts. This dessert was supposedly created in 1898 for the Prince of Wales, the future Edward VII, at the Café de Paris in Monte Carlo. It was named by the prince himself, after his beautiful companion, Suzette.

Crêpes

(MAKES 18 TO 20)

- 2 eggs
- ½ cup (1 stick) melted butter
- 1 cup milk
- 1 teaspoon vanilla extract
- ¼ cup water
- ½ teaspoon salt
- 1¼ cups all-purpose flour
- A little oil for frying

- 8 tablespoons (1 stick) unsalted butter
- ½ cup sugar
- Juice of 1 orange
- 3 ounces brandy
- 3 ounces Grand Marnier

1 Put all crêpe ingredients except oil in blender container and blend until smooth, stirring down a couple of times if necessary. The batter should just lightly coat a spoon. If it is too thick, stir in a little more water.

2 Lightly grease a small skillet with a paper towel dipped in oil. Heat skillet. When hot, thinly cover the bottom of the skillet with batter. When edge of crêpe turns brown and small holes appear (about 1 minute), turn crêpe and cook for about 30 seconds longer. Turn crêpe out onto a paper towel and repeat until all batter is used. Set aside 8 crêpes; refrigerate or freeze the rest.

3 Put butter and sugar in a skillet or chafing dish at the table. Cook over moderate heat, stirring constantly, until sugar is caramelized. When it turns amber, squeeze in a little juice from the orange and continue to stir. Don't add large amounts of juice at one time or the mixture will get lumpy.

4 When all the juice has been added and sauce is smooth, simmer over low heat. Add the crêpes, one by one, placing each flat in the pan and spooning the sauce over. Fold crêpes in half and in half again to form triangles. When all the crêpes have been sauced and folded, add brandy and Grand Marnier and ignite. Spoon the flaming sauce over the crêpes until the flames are extinguished.

5 Serve each person 2 crêpes and a little of the sauce.

Note: Many of New Orleans' popular flaming desserts are made with crêpes tableside. The dramatic presentation in restaurants may intimidate people into thinking they are too difficult to make at home. Actually, they are very simple, and the crêpes can be made earlier in the day, rolled in waxed paper to keep moist, and refrigerated until needed. Crêpes can be made in large batches and frozen for months; they defrost in only a few minutes.

Crêpes Kovacs

SERVES 8

This is our most popular crêpe dessert. The crêpes are filled with an orange-rum-raisin cream cheese mixture, topped with a flaming sauce of pecans, raisins, orange marmalade, and Triple Sec, and served over custard. Divine!

16 Crêpes (page 164)

Filling

- 1 pound cream cheese, softened
- Juice of 1 orange
- 1 tablespoon light or dark rum
- ½ cup sugar
- ⅓ cup raisins

Custard Sauce

- 2 tablespoons (¼ stick) unsalted butter
- 1 cup heavy cream
- 1 egg, fork-beaten
- ½ cup sugar

Topping

- 6 tablespoons (¾ stick) unsalted butter
- 1 cup chopped pecans
- 1 cup raisins
- 1 cup orange marmalade
- 1 tablespoon cinnamon

½ cup Triple Sec

1 ■ *To make filling:* Put cream cheese, orange juice, rum, and sugar in bowl of electric mixer and beat until smooth and creamy. Fold in raisins and chill until stiff.

2 ■ Spread each crêpe with about 2 tablespoons of filling and roll up, jelly-roll fashion. Set aside.

3 ■ *To make custard sauce:* Heat butter in a skillet or chafing dish. Add cream, stirring. Add the egg and sugar, stirring constantly. If the pan gets too hot take it off the heat, but keep stirring. (If the mixture gets too hot you'll have scrambled egg rather than custard.) As you stir, the sauce will thicken and reduce to about half its original volume. When thick enough to coat a spoon, set aside but keep warm.

4 ■ *To make the topping:* Melt butter in a separate skillet or crêpe pan. Add pecans and raisins and stir gently until they are warm. Add marmalade and cinnamon and stir and mash with a spoon.

5 ■ Place crêpes one by one in pan and turn once to heat them on all sides. When warm through, add the Triple Sec and flame. Serve as soon as the flame burns out.

6 *To serve:* Cover bottom of each dessert plate with ¼ cup of the custard. Arrange 2 crêpes in center of custard. Finish with a spoonful of topping.

Lemon Crêpes

SERVES 6

A delicious light dessert. Thin crêpes are filled with a mixture of cream cheese, sugar, rum, and grated lemon rind and covered with a lovely lemon butter sauce.

Filling

- 1 pound cream cheese, softened
- ⅔ cup sugar
- Juice of 1 medium lemon
- 1 tablespoon light rum
- 1 tablespoon grated lemon rind

Lemon Butter Sauce

- ½ pound (2 sticks) unsalted butter
- ¼ cup sugar
- Juice of 3 medium lemons, or about ½ cup lemon juice
- 1 tablespoon grated lemon rind

- 12 crêpes (page 164)

1 *To make filling:* In bowl of an electric mixer beat cream cheese until fluffy. Gradually beat in sugar and remaining ingredients. Set aside.

2 *To make sauce:* Melt butter in a small saucepan over low heat. Add sugar and stir until dissolved. Stir in lemon juice and rind. Set aside.

3 *To serve:* Spoon about 3 tablespoons filling in a long strip down center of each crêpe; roll up, jelly-roll fashion, and tuck ends under on seam side. In a large skillet or chafing dish, heat lemon butter sauce without letting the butter brown. Put crêpes in the pan side by side, seam side up. Heat for 1 to 2 minutes. Turn seam side down. Add the brandy, swirl pan to coat the crêpes with it, and ignite.

4 Put 2 crêpes in each dessert dish and spoon some of the sauce over them.

French Bread Pudding with Clear Rum Sauce

SERVES 6

Originally devised as a way to use leftover stale French bread, bread pudding has become one of the most popular classic New Orleans desserts. Every cook has his own secret recipe. Commander's version is served hot from the oven with a thin rum sauce. If you have any left over, try the recipe for bread pudding soufflé that follows.

- 1 cup sugar
- 8 tablespoons (1 stick) butter, softened
- 5 eggs, beaten
- 1 pint (2 cups) heavy cream
- Dash of cinnamon
- 1 tablespoon vanilla extract
- ¼ cup raisins
- 12 slices, each 1 inch thick, of fresh or stale French bread

Clear Rum Sauce

- 1 cup sugar
- 2¼ cups water
- 1 cinnamon stick or 1 teaspoon ground cinnamon
- 1 tablespoon unsalted butter
- ½ teaspoon cornstarch
- 1 tablespoon light or dark rum

1 ■ Preheat oven to 350°.

2 ■ In a large bowl cream together the sugar and butter. Add eggs, cream, cinnamon, vanilla, and raisins, mixing well. Pour into a 9-inch-square pan 1¾ inches deep.

3 ■ Arrange bread slices flat in the egg mixture and let stand for 5 minutes to soak up some of the liquid. Turn bread over and let stand for 10 minutes longer. Then push bread down so that most of it is covered by the egg mixture. Do not break the bread.

4 ■ Set pan in a larger pan filled with water to ½ inch from top. Cover with aluminum foil. Bake for 45 to 50 minutes, uncovering pudding for the last 10 minutes to brown the top. When done, the custard should still be soft, not firm.

5 ■ *To make the sauce:* In a medium-size saucepan combine sugar, 2 cups water, cinnamon, and butter and bring to a boil. Stir in cornstarch blended with remaining ¼ cup water and simmer, stirring, until sauce is clear. Remove from heat and add rum. Sauce will be thin.

6 ■ *To serve:* Spoon the pudding onto dessert plates and pass the sauce separately.

■ ***Note:*** The rum sauce is also good with fresh pineapple. Heat pineapple "wheels" in it (do not cook, however), then serve on a plate lightly covered with the sauce.

Bread Pudding Soufflé with Whiskey Sauce

SERVES 8

We love bread pudding and decided to bring it up to today's Haute Creole by making it into a soufflé. It has become a very popular dessert. We served it at Commander's 100th Anniversary Dinner for the 2nd Symposium on American Cuisine. Time your dinner carefully, as this dessert must be served the moment it has finished baking. Spoon it onto individual dessert plates and top with a hot whiskey sauce.

- 2½ cups French Bread Pudding (page 168)
- 6 egg yolks
- ½ cup granulated sugar
- 6 egg whites
- ½ cup confectioners' sugar

- Unsalted butter
- Granulated sugar

Whiskey Sauce

- 1 cup sugar
- 1 cup heavy cream
- 1 cinnamon stick or a dash of ground cinnamon
- 1 tablespoon unsalted butter
- ½ teaspoon cornstarch
- 1 tablespoon bourbon
- ¼ cup additional water

1 Make bread pudding and set aside 2½ cups.

2 *To make the soufflé:* Preheat oven to 375°.

3 Put egg yolks and sugar in top of a double boiler. Whip over simmering water with a whisk until frothy and shiny. Mix yolk mixture with reserved bread pudding until smooth.

4 Beat egg whites until frothy. Gradually add confectioners' sugar, beating constantly until the resulting meringue stands in stiff peaks. Gently fold egg whites into bread pudding mixture.

5 Butter and lightly sugar a 1½-quart soufflé dish. Turn soufflé mixture into the dish, filling it three quarters full. Wipe lip of the soufflé dish clean and bake for 35 to 40 minutes.

6 *To make the sauce:* While soufflé is baking, in a saucepan combine sugar, 1 cup cream, cinnamon, and butter. Bring to a boil. Add in the cornstarch mixed with the ¼ cup water and cook, stirring, until sauce is clear. Remove from heat and stir in whiskey.

7 *To serve:* Remove soufflé from oven and serve immediately, with the sauce in a separate bowl on the side.

Café au Lait Soufflé

SERVES 4

New Orleans' rich café au lait is a local institution, served at breakfast and at the French Market with beignets. We first saw a version of this dessert served at the Four Seasons restaurant in New York, and loved it so much we had to make our own. Use a strong instant coffee or powdered espresso of your choice to flavor the soufflé, and serve the coffee-flavored cream sauce in a separate bowl.

- 1 tablespoon unsalted butter
- 1 tablespoon all-purpose flour
- 1 cup milk
- ½ cup plus 1 tablespoon sugar
- Pinch of salt
- 3 tablespoons instant coffee
- 4 egg yolks
- ½ teaspoon vanilla extract
- 4 egg whites

Sauce

- 2 cups heavy cream
- 2 teaspoons instant coffee
- 2 ounces coffee liqueur
- 1 tablespoon sugar
- 1 teaspoon vanilla extract
- 6 egg yolks

1 ■ Preheat oven to 400°.

2 ■ Heat butter and flour in a heavy saucepan over gentle heat, stirring until smooth. Gradually stir in milk and cook, stirring, until thick and smooth. Remove from heat, add ½ cup sugar, salt, and instant coffee, and stir until sugar and coffee are dissolved. Beat in egg yolks and vanilla extract and set aside.

3 ■ Beat egg whites and 1 tablespoon sugar until the mixture stands in soft peaks. Add a fifth of the beaten egg whites to the yolk mixture to lighten it and fold in thoroughly. Add remaining egg whites and fold in gently and briefly.

4 ■ Spoon into a buttered 1-quart soufflé dish and bake in the hot oven for 12 to 15 minutes. The soufflé should be a little soft *(baveuse)* in the center.

5 ■ *To make the sauce:* Put all sauce ingredients except egg yolks in a saucepan and bring to a simmer. Cook, stirring, until coffee and sugar are dissolved. Remove from heat and whisk in egg yolks.

6 ■ *To serve:* Serve soufflé immediately upon taking it from the oven. Spoon onto plates and pass the sauce separately.

Crêpes Soufflé Praline

SERVES 8

People loved our praline candy and praline parfait so much we knew this Haute Creole version would be very popular too. Delicate crêpes are filled with a light meringue-custard mixture, flavored with pecans, nutmeg, and cinnamon, covered with additional custard, and sprinkled with more pecans on top. The crêpes are baked until they rise and the pecans begin to brown.

16 Crêpes (page 164)

Meringue

1¼ cups egg whites (about 6)
2 cups confectioners' sugar
1 tablespoon light or dark rum

Custard

2 cups milk
2 eggs
1½ teaspoons vanilla extract
½ teaspoon dark corn syrup
½ teaspoon ground cinnamon
½ teaspoon grated nutmeg
1½ cups chopped pecans

Topping

1 cup pecan halves, chopped

1 *To make meringue:* Beat egg whites with an electric mixer until frothy. Gradually beat in sugar and continue to beat until meringue forms soft peaks. Add rum and beat until meringue forms stiff peaks. Measure 1 cup for the custard and reserve the rest.

2 *Make custard:* In top of double boiler combine milk and eggs. Stir in vanilla extract and corn syrup. Cook over simmering water until custard just coats the spoon. Remove from heat and stir in cinnamon, nutmeg, and chopped pecans. Fold in the cup of meringue. Set aside.

3 Preheat oven to 425°.

4 *To serve:* Using ovenproof serving plates, put 2 tablespoons custard mixture on each crêpe and top with ½ cup of the reserved meringue. Fold crêpe carefully around filling and place seam side down. Put 2 crêpes on each plate. Pour additional custard sauce over crêpes and sprinkle with pecan halves. Bake in bottom half of the oven until pecans begin to brown, about 7 minutes. Serve immediately.

French Vanilla Ice Cream

MAKES 2 QUARTS

All our ice creams and sorbets are homemade. The French vanilla is particularly creamy and rich, with a high percentage of butterfat. It serves as the basis for many of our cool summer desserts.

- 1 quart milk
- 1 vanilla bean, halved lengthwise
- 2½ cups sugar
- 6 egg yolks, beaten
- 1 tablespoon vanilla extract
- 1 pint (2 cups) heavy cream, whipped

1 ■ Heat milk in a saucepan. Just before it boils, remove from heat and stir in vanilla bean and sugar. Stir until sugar is dissolved. Cool slightly, then stir in egg yolks.

2 ■ Scrape the brown pulp from inside the vanilla bean into the milk mixture. (This is the heart of the bean, where the real flavor is.) Stir in vanilla extract and whipped cream. Freeze in freezer container for 6 to 8 hours, or until hard.

■ ***Note:*** For a smoother texture, pour into container of hand-churned or electric ice cream maker, following manufacturer's directions, and churn until stiff. Then pack into freezer container and let ripen overnight in freezer.

■ ***Variation:*** Add 1 quart brandied cherries, drained, and 1 cup bittersweet chocolate bits to the ice cream before freezing for a rich holiday treat.

Champagne Ice

MAKES 1 QUART

This is chef Gerhard Brill's version of a champagne ice. It is very light and refreshing. Puréed fruit gives this ice added body and texture.

- 3 cups water
- 1½ cups sugar
- ½ cup lemon juice
- ½ cup pineapple juice
- ½ cup champagne
- ½ cup purée of peeled plums (Santa Rosa are good)

1 ■ Bring water and sugar to a boil and boil until sugar is dissolved, about 3 minutes. Let cool.

2 ■ Stir in rest of ingredients, pour into a container, and freeze for 3 to 4 hours. For a fine snowy texture, stir every 30 minutes until frozen.

Praline Parfait

SERVES 6

We took the classic Creole praline candy, which everyone loves, and decided to keep the sauce liquid and serve it over vanilla ice cream. With whipped cream and chopped roasted pecans, it's a real indulgence. Praline sauce can be kept in the refrigerator for as long as two weeks, so making this is an easy last-minute dessert.

1½ cups white corn syrup
1½ cups dark corn syrup
1½ cups chopped roasted pecans
1 teaspoon vanilla extract
Dash of nutmeg
Dash of cinnamon
12 scoops French Vanilla Ice Cream (page 172)
1 cup heavy cream, whipped

Garnish

6 maraschino cherries

1 Mix together the corn syrups, pecans, vanilla extract, nutmeg, and cinnamon. Put 2 tablespoons of this praline sauce in bottom of each parfait dish.

2 Add 2 scoops of ice cream and top with a generous lacing of praline sauce.

3 Top the sauce with a lavish spoonful of whipped cream and garnish with a cherry.

Note: There will probably be some sauce left over for use another time.

Avocado Cream Parfait

SERVES 6

A creamy, unusual summer dessert, this is a beautiful pale jade color and has a strong nutty avocado flavor. Be sure to use a very ripe avocado.

- 1 very ripe medium avocado
- 2½ tablespoons fresh lime juice
- 6 tablespoons granulated sugar
- ½ cup heavy cream
- 1½ teaspoons vanilla extract
- 4 cups French Vanilla Ice Cream (page 172), slightly softened

1 ■ Peel avocado, remove pit, and slice coarsely into container of an electric blender.

2 ■ Add lime juice and purée until smooth.

3 ■ Add sugar, cream, and vanilla extract and blend again until smooth.

4 ■ Remove from container and mix thoroughly into the softened ice cream.

5 ■ Pile ¾ cup of the avocado cream into each parfait glass and put glasses in the freezer for about 5½ hours, or until hard.

Strawberries Romanoff

SERVES 4

Made with the freshest, sweetest, ripest strawberries in season and rich, rich homemade vanilla ice cream, this simple dish reaches aristocratic heights. Reserve the biggest, most beautiful berries for garnishing. We always put a big silver bowl or baskets of strawberries in the dining room as a reminder and decorative accompaniment.

- 24 very ripe medium strawberries
- 2 teaspoons sugar
- 8 scoops French Vanilla Ice Cream (page 172)
- 2 cups heavy cream, whipped
- 4 ounces Triple Sec or Grand Marnier

Garnish

- 4 large, perfect strawberries

1 ■ With a fork, crush berries with sugar in a mixing bowl.

2 ■ Add ice cream and whipped cream and fold all together gently.

3 ■ Fold in Triple Sec or Grand Marnier and spoon into wineglasses.

4 ■ Garnish each serving with a berry. Serve immediately.

Flaming Baked Alaska

SERVES 2

This classic ice cream dessert is really very simple to create—just ice cream and pound cake topped with meringue—but it makes a dramatic and impressive presentation, especially flamed with brandy as we do it.

- 1 slice pound cake, ¼ inch thick
- ¼ cup orange marmalade
- 3 scoops French Vanilla Ice Cream (page 172)

Meringue

- ⅔ cup egg whites (about 4)
- ⅛ teaspoon cream of tartar
- 1 cup confectioners' sugar
- 2 tablespoons light or dark rum

- 2 tablespoons brandy

1 Put pound cake on a heatproof serving plate and spread orange marmalade evenly on top. Put the ice cream on top of the marmalade and put plate in the freezer while preparing the meringue.

2 *To make the meringue:* Beat egg whites and cream of tartar with an electric mixer until frothy. Gradually beat in confectioners' sugar and continue to beat until meringue stands in stiff, glossy peaks. Fold in rum.

3 Spoon meringue into a pastry bag fitted with a large fluted pastry tube and pipe out meringue in circles or other decorative pattern, completely covering ice cream and cake. Freeze again until completely hard.

4 *To serve:* Preheat oven to 400°. Put frozen dessert in the very hot oven for 2 to 4 minutes, or until meringue is tinged with brown. Heat brandy in a small saucepan, ignite, and ladle the flaming brandy over the dessert. Serve immediately.

Celebration Dessert

SERVES 4

We had been searching for an interesting party dessert to replace the birthday cake customers frequently ask restaurants to serve. One day we went to see a movie, Who Is Killing the Great Chefs of Europe?, *in which the chef at Buckingham Palace was making a marvelous chocolate bombe, and it inspired us to create the celebration dessert. Our version consists of a raspberry mousse center surrounded by vanilla ice cream, covered with a thick layer of chocolate frosting. It is made especially festive by piping the rich chocolate frosting down the sides of the bombe with a fluted pastry tube in the form of overlapping ribbons, and piping stars around the base. When it comes to the table you can hear the oohs and aahs. This is an especially popular dessert with chocolate lovers. You can make it in a medium-size bombe or charlotte russe mold (5-cup capacity) or, as here, in individual cups.*

16 ounces (1 pint) French Vanilla Ice Cream, softened (page 172)

Raspberry Filling

1 pint (2 cups) heavy cream
¾ cup Raspberry Sauce (page 178), chilled

Chocolate Frosting

2 cups whipping cream
½ cup sugar
¾ cup semisweet cocoa powder

1 Line the inside of four 10-ounce paper cups with softened ice cream, molding it around the inside of the cup about ½ inch thick, leaving the center empty. Freeze until ice cream is hard.

2 *To make raspberry filling:* Beat cream until it forms stiff peaks. Add raspberry sauce and beat again to stiff peaks. Fill the center of the cups with this filling and freeze again until very hard.

3 Turn the paper cups upside down under cold running water until they release the dessert, and quickly slip onto individual chilled plates. Freeze again until edges harden.

4 *To make chocolate frosting:* Beat cream and sugar with an electric mixer until very stiff. Gradually beat in cocoa powder. Spoon into a pastry bag fitted with a fluted star tube and pipe the frosting over the dessert and down the sides in a decorative pattern. Pipe out small stars or "kisses" all around the base. Store in freezer until ready to serve.

Amaretto Freeze

MAKES 1 SERVING

A simple and delicious dessert using the almond-flavored Italian liqueur, the amaretto freeze is cool and refreshing. Naturally, it's better with homemade ice cream, but you can use a rich store-bought variety. The ice cream should be blended with crushed ice and amaretto until it is the consistency of a thick malted. Serve in chilled wine goblets with almond cookies or macaroons, garnished with fresh strawberries.

- 8 to 10 ounces French Vanilla Ice Cream (a heaping cup) (page 172)
- 1½ ounces amaretto liqueur
- ½ scoop crushed ice

Garnish

- Fresh strawberries

1 Put all ingredients in blender container and blend until well mixed and the consistency of a thick malted milk shake.

2 Serve it in 10- to 12-ounce goblets and garnish with strawberries.

Creole Cream Cheese Ice Cream

MAKES 2½ QUARTS

Creole cream cheese is a New Orleans favorite, especially for breakfast, with fresh fruit. It is something like farmer cheese, only richer and creamier. It is only available locally, however, so if you cannot get it, skip this recipe.

- 5 11-ounce cartons Creole cream cheese
- 1 pint (2 cups) milk
- 1 pint (2 cups) heavy cream
- 3 cups sugar
- 2 egg yolks
- 3 teaspoons vanilla extract

Sauce

- 2 11-ounce cartons Creole cream cheese
- 1 cup heavy cream
- Juice of 1 lemon
- 1 teaspoon vanilla extract

1 Mash cream cheese through a colander to eliminate any large pieces. Add milk, cream, sugar, and egg yolks and beat thoroughly. Add vanilla extract. Stir well and freeze in an ice cream freezer, following manufacturer's directions.

2 *To make sauce:* Mash the cream cheese as described above. Add remaining ingredients and beat until smooth and well blended.

3 *To serve:* Ladle sauce over ice cream in dessert dishes.

Chocolate Mousse

SERVES 6 TO 8

Commander's has three favorite mousse desserts, which we rotate: chocolate, white chocolate with raspberry sauce, and lemon.

- 2 ounces unsweetened chocolate
- 1½ cups heavy cream
- 8 egg whites
- ⅛ teaspoon cream of tartar
- ½ cup confectioners' sugar

Garnish

Chocolate shavings

1 ■ Melt chocolate in a double boiler over simmering water.

2 ■ In a mixing bowl beat cream until it forms stiff peaks.

3 ■ In another bowl, beat egg whites with cream of tartar at medium speed until frothy. Gradually beat in confectioners' sugar and beat until meringue stands in stiff peaks but is still glossy.

4 ■ Gently fold together meringue and whipped cream. Fold in chocolate and continue to fold until chocolate is evenly distributed.

5 ■ Spoon into individual mousse or custard cups, garnish with chocolate shavings, and chill for 2 to 3 hours before serving.

White Chocolate Mousse

SERVES 6 TO 8

Raspberry Sauce

- 2 cups fresh raspberries, puréed
- ½ cup sugar
- ¼ cup brandy

- 6 ounces white chocolate
- 1½ cups heavy cream
- 8 egg whites
- ⅛ teaspoon cream of tartar
- ¾ cup confectioners' sugar

Garnish

Chocolate shavings

1 ■ *To make raspberry sauce:* In a small saucepan combine raspberries and sugar. Bring to a boil, reduce heat, and simmer for 2 minutes. Add brandy and flame. Set aside to cool while you make the mousse.

2 ■ Melt chocolate in a double boiler over simmering water and set aside.

3 ■ Beat cream until it stands in stiff peaks.

4 ■ In another bowl beat egg whites with cream of tartar at medium

speed until frothy. Gradually beat in confectioners' sugar, and continue to beat until the meringue stands in stiff peaks but is still glossy.

5 ■ Gently fold together meringue and whipped cream. Gradually fold in melted chocolate.

6 ■ Spoon 2 tablespoons of raspberry sauce into four 8-ounce wineglasses. Fill with mousse and garnish with chocolate shavings. Refrigerate for several hours until ready to serve.

Lemon Mousse

SERVES 4

- 1½ cups heavy cream
- 1 cup sugar
- 6 tablespoons strained lemon juice
- 8 egg whites
- ⅛ teaspoon cream of tartar

Garnish

- 4 thin slices lemon
- Zest of 1 lemon

1 ■ Whip the cream, gradually adding half the sugar. When the cream begins to thicken, beat in lemon juice, and continue to beat until it stands in stiff peaks.

2 ■ Whip egg whites with cream of tartar until they stand in soft peaks. Gradually beat in remaining sugar, and beat until meringue forms stiff peaks. Do not overbeat—egg whites should remain glossy.

3 ■ Fold meringue into the lemon cream. Spoon into four 8-ounce serving glasses and chill until ready to serve.

4 ■ *To serve:* Garnish with lemon slice and lemon zest.

Caramel Cup Custard

SERVES 6

A classic French recipe brought over by the original New Orleans settlers, this rich, smooth egg custard with caramel sauce is light and elegant, suitable for any occasion, plain or fancy, luncheon or dinner. Chill for at least an hour before serving.

Caramelized Sugar

(MAKES ½ CUP)

1 cup sugar

1½ tablespoons water

Custard

2 cups milk
3 eggs
2 egg yolks
½ cup sugar
¼ teaspoon nutmeg
1 tablespoon vanilla extract

1 ■ Preheat oven to 350°.

2 ■ *To caramelize the sugar:* In a small skillet over medium heat, combine sugar and water. Stir until sugar caramelizes and turns a rich brown. Remove from heat and continue to stir to keep the sugar from burning. Spoon 1 tablespoon apiece into the bottom of six 4-ounce custard cups.

3 ■ *To make the custard:* Heat milk until hot but not boiling. In a large mixing bowl beat remaining ingredients until well blended. Gradually beat in the hot milk. Ladle ½ cup into each custard cup. Put cups in a deep baking pan and fill with enough hot water to reach about ¾ up sides of custard cups. Bake until knife inserted in center comes out clean, 45 to 50 minutes. Cool, then chill.

Floating Island

SERVES 6

A vision of ethereal meringues floating in custard, topped with caramelized sugar and crushed pecans, this dessert is especially popular during the holidays. A nice presentation is to bring it to the table in a lovely crystal or ceramic bowl, then spoon it onto individual plates at the table.

- 4 eggs, separated
- ½ cup confectioners' sugar
- 2 cups milk
- 2 cups heavy cream
- ½ cup granulated sugar
- 1 tablespoon cornstarch
- 2 tablespoons light rum
- 1 teaspoon vanilla extract
- ½ cup Caramelized Sugar (page 179)
- ½ cup finely chopped pecans

1 Beat egg whites until frothy. Gradually beat in confectioners' sugar. Beat until meringue is very stiff but still glossy. Set aside.

2 Over medium heat, bring milk and cream to a gentle simmer. With an ice cream scoop, scoop balls of meringue into the simmering milk. Poach balls for 2 to 3 minutes, rolling over with a spoon dipped in hot water. When all sides are cooked, lift out from milk with a slotted spoon and set aside.

3 Add sugar to the milk and cream remaining in the pan and bring back to the simmer. Combine egg yolks and cornstarch with about 1 cup of the hot milk mixture and return to the pan, stirring constantly. Cook, stirring, for about 2 minutes, or until custard thickens, being careful not to let it boil. When smooth and thickened, remove from heat. It should be the consistency of lightly whipped cream.

4 Stir in rum and vanilla extract. Let cool, then refrigerate until cold.

5 *To serve:* Stir custard gently and spoon about ½ cup into each dish. Set a meringue ball on top and over it swirl about 1 teaspoon caramelized sugar. Sprinkle with nuts.

Poached Pears in Pistachio Sauce

SERVES 6

This dessert was first served at Commander's for a dinner for the Chevaliers du Tastevin gourmet society. Fresh firm pears poached in sweet dessert wine are rolled in semisweet chocolate shavings and served on a platter covered with a cream-enriched reduction of the pear-wine sauce, studded with pistachio nuts. This has become a popular elegant dessert for private parties, and makes a nice complement to a fine sauterne.

- 2 lemons
- 2 oranges
- 6 ripe but firm pears (Bartlett, Bosc, Comice, or Packham)
- 3 cups sweet dessert wine (such as sauterne)
- ½ cup sugar
- 2 pints (4 cups) heavy cream
- ½ cup shelled pistachio nuts
- 6 ounces semisweet chocolate, shaved

1 ■ With a lemon zester or vegetable peeler, remove the thin colored rinds from the fruit without including any of the white underneath. (Use the fruit for some other purpose.)

2 ■ Core and peel pears, without removing steams. Set aside.

3 ■ Pour wine into a large shallow saucepan, add sugar and fruit zest, bring to a boil, and simmer for 3 minutes.

4 ■ With slotted spoon, lower pears into the syrup so they are partially covered, return syrup to a simmer, and cook for 5 to 8 minutes, basting occasionally, until pears are tender but still firm. Remove pears and keep warm.

5 ■ Continue to boil syrup rapidly until reduced by half. Add cream and continue to boil until sauce is reduced by one quarter. Add nuts.

6 ■ Pour sauce into a shallow serving dish. One at a time, roll pears in the shaved chocolate and put in the sauce. Serve while sauce is still warm.

Pecan Pie

MAKES ONE 8-INCH PIE

Soul-satisfying and incredibly rich and sweet, pecan pie is a New Orleans tradition and a favorite dessert since the first days of pecan growing in Louisiana. Serve it at room temperature, or hot with fresh whipped cream, ice cream, or just a dot of butter.

Basic Piecrust

- 1¼ cups all-purpose flour
- ¼ tablespoon salt
- Dash of sugar
- 8 tablespoons (1 stick) unsalted butter
- ¼ cup vegetable shortening
- 3 to 4 tablespoons ice water

- ⅓ cup butter
- ¾ cup firmly packed light brown sugar
- 3 eggs
- ½ cup light corn syrup
- 1 cup chopped pecans
- 1 teaspoon vanilla extract
- ¼ teaspoon salt

Garnish

- Pecan halves

1 *To make and bake pie shell:* Preheat oven to 375°.

2 Sift flour, salt, and sugar into mixing bowl. Cut in butter and shortening with pastry blender or two knives until mixture looks like coarse cornmeal. Add water and mix with a fork until dough holds together. Shape into a rough ball and chill for 30 minutes.

3 Roll out on a floured surface into a circle 2 inches in diameter larger than the pie plate and ⅛ inch thick. Transfer to pan by rolling dough onto rolling pin and unrolling over pan. Ease gently into pan, trim edge, and flute. Prick bottom and sides with a fork and bake for 8 to 10 minutes until golden brown. Do not turn oven off.

4 Meanwhile, cream together butter and brown sugar. Beat in eggs, one at a time. Stir in corn syrup, pecans, vanilla extract, and salt. Fill baked pie shell and decorate top with pecan halves. Bake for 30 minutes.

Note: Dough can be wrapped and refrigerated for several days before using or it can be frozen.

Chocolate-Coated Chocolate Truffles

MAKES 5 DOZEN

Truffles, bourbon balls, and pralines—these sweets are wonderful after dessert and with coffee. Put a variety of them on a decorative platter and watch them disappear!

3 pounds semisweet chocolate, cut into pieces
2 cups heavy cream
6 tablespoons (¾ stick) unsalted butter
⅓ cup granulated sugar
Confectioners' sugar for dusting

1 ■ Melt 2 pounds chocolate over simmering water. Combine cream, butter, and granulated sugar and bring to a boil. Mix melted chocolate with the cream mixture and chill until very thick.

2 ■ Spoon filling into a pastry bag fitted with a #8 round tube. Press out small balls, the size of walnuts, and chill until firm. Dust with confectioners' sugar and set aside.

3 ■ Melt remaining chocolate in the top of a double boiler over simmering water. Let cool enough to handle. Spoon some chocolate into the palms of your hands and roll the chocolate balls between the coated palms. Chill balls until firm and then coat again with melted chocolate. Store in refrigerator.

Pecan Bourbon Balls

MAKES ABOUT 20

- 2½ cups crushed vanilla wafer crumbs
- 2 tablespoons cocoa
- 1 cup confectioners' sugar
- 1 cup chopped pecans
- 3 tablespoons corn syrup
- ¼ cup bourbon

Garnish

Confectioners' sugar

1 In a mixing bowl combine crumbs, cocoa, confectioners' sugar, and nuts. Stir in corn syrup and bourbon.

2 Form into 1-inch balls and roll in confectioners' sugar to coat. Refrigerate.

Pralines

MAKES 3 DOZEN

- 1 quart heavy cream
- 3 cups sugar
- 1½ pounds chopped pecans (6 cups)
- Juice of 1 lemon

1 In a heavy saucepan slowly simmer cream and sugar over low heat until the mixture becomes golden brown in color and reaches the soft-ball stage.* Add pecans and lemon juice and continue to cook until the soft-ball stage is reached again.

2 Drop from a large kitchen spoon onto an oiled baking sheet or a marble slab moistened with water. Spread each cake out with back of spoon to about ¼ inch thick and 4 to 5 inches in diameter. Let harden, then lift from plate or slab with a spatula.

3 Pralines will keep for 2 weeks in a covered tin at room temperature.

* The soft-ball stage is reached when a small amount of syrup dropped into ice water holds its shape without separating into threads.

Café Noir

A good Creole cook never boils coffee, but drips it slowly until all the flavor is extracted. (The modern Chemex and other drip coffeemakers using paper filters work very well.) Allow 1 rounded tablespoon coffee per cup, pour in freshly boiled water (overboiled water spoils the flavor), wait for the rich, fragrant aroma to arise, and serve in fine china cups.

Café au Lait

Café au lait is a New Orleans institution, a thick, rich coffee concoction natives drink at breakfast, all day long, and after dinner with sugar, instead of dessert. Usually, equal parts of milk (or cream), heated just to the boiling point, and coffee are used, though this is a matter of taste. It's nice sometimes to serve it with a little coffee ceremony, simultaneously pouring coffee from a pot in one hand and boiling milk or cream from a pot in the other hand.

Café Brûlot

SERVES 2

As a dramatic climax to an elegant dinner we serve a flaming café brûlot after dessert. The heady combination of coffee, brandy and rum, cinnamon and cloves, orange and lemon peel makes a grand finale. We make a festive presentation using a special brûlot bowl: The ribbon of gold-blue flame follows the lemon peel spiral as the mixture is ladled in the air for dramatic effect. If you plan to do this for guests, practice the technique first. Special brûlot sets of bowls, ladles, and cups are available, and are a traditional wedding gift in New Orleans. Café brûlot can also be made in a chafing dish and served in demitasse cups.

- 1 lemon
- 1 orange
- 2 dozen whole cloves
- 2 cinnamon sticks
- 1½ ounces Triple Sec
- 1 ounce brandy
- 1½ cups strong hot black coffee

1 ■ Peel lemon with one continuous motion so that peel is in long spiral (peel over brûlot bowl so that any juices go into the bowl). Peel orange in the same fashion. Insert cloves into the spiraled orange and lemon peel at 1-inch intervals so that they are studded with cloves.

2 ■ Light a Sterno stove.

3 ■ In a brûlot bowl, place the cinnamon sticks. Add Triple Sec and brandy and stir together. Carefully ignite brandy. Stir, lifting the ladle high in the air. A ribbon of golden-blue flame follows the motion. Mount lemon and orange peels on a fork so that you can hold them over the brûlot bowl for flaming. Ladle ignited brandy over the peels.

4 Gradually add coffee, pouring around the edge of the bowl so that a hissing sound is heard, and continue mixing until flame dies out. With a fork, squeeze a small amount of orange juice into the bowl to sweeten the coffee.

5 Pour into demitasse cups with the brûlot ladle and serve.

Café Pierre

SERVES 2

This is a fabulous dessert coffee, created by one of the captains in the restaurant, named Pierre, who made it for our sister Adelaide, who then began to serve it to her friends. Suddenly, it became very popular in New Orleans. It is very rich, with brandy, Kahlua, and Galliano topped with whipped cream—a dessert in itself. It is also a treat to watch the captains make it tableside, rimming the glass first with lime, then with sugar, which crystallizes when the brandy is ignited. At home, do not *use fine crystal, which may break with the heat of the flame.*

- 2 ounces brandy
- 2 ounces Kahlua
- 2 ounces Galliano
- 4 ounces whipped cream
- 16 ounces hot black coffee
- 1 fresh lime, cut into wedges
- Sugar

Using a heatproof 10-ounce all-purpose wineglass, rim the glass with lime and sugar. Hold glass over flame, caramelizing sugar, then pour brandy in glass, carefully ignite, and flame. Add Galliano and flame. Add coffee and float whipped cream. Use a ladle and add Kahlua, flaming, over the whipped cream.

Irish Coffee

SERVES 1

This rich, old-fashioned coffee drink became popular in the United States in the late 1940s and 50s, when people started drinking it instead of eating dessert. It was served in the airport in Dublin, and Americans visiting Ireland grew so fond of it they got their local bartenders to learn how to make it. The Brennan family, being Irish, is especially fond of this drink.

- 1 ounce Irish whiskey
- 1½ teaspoons Simple Syrup (page 4) or sugar to taste
- 6 ounces strong hot black coffee
- Heavy cream

1 In an 8-ounce glass, put whiskey and syrup. Stir. Pour coffee to within one inch of top of glass.

2 Top with heavy cream.

Lagniappe: Seasonings, Stocks, and Sauces

Lagniappe is a term used chiefly in Southern Louisiana and Southeast Texas to refer to "a little something extra" given to a customer by way of good measure. So, here, in addition to Commander's basic dishes, we are including the recipes for the special Creole seasonings, stocks, and sauces that are the lifeblood of New Orleans cooking. We are absolutely intrepid about using our spirited sauces and seasonings on everything from steak to eggs.

Certainly the most important part of any dish, these seasonings, sauces, and stocks contain the essence of the Creole taste. This is especially true of the new Haute Creole cuisine, which relies on repeated reductions to achieve rich and intense flavors. Many of these recipes are New Orleans versions of classic French sauces, but prepared with more seasoning—garlic, cayenne pepper, Worcestershire sauce, or Louisiana Red Hot Sauce—than their French counterparts. For instance, meunière is the classic French butter sauce used on fish; at Commander's we "Creolize" it with garlic, onion, Worcestershire, tomato, oregano, cayenne, and pepper! It's especially delicious on fresh trout with roasted pecans.

You will notice that what we call "Creole meat seasoning" and "Creole seafood seasoning" are used again and again in these recipes. Basically, these are mixtures of dried garlic, black and cayenne peppers, salt, paprika, dried onion, and herbs. With jars of these two seasonings on the shelf in your kitchen, you can quickly and easily "Creolize" many different dishes, your own as well as the ones in this book.

Preparation of stocks and sauces is sometimes the most time-consuming part of a dish. So if you plan to do lots of Creole cooking, it would be wise to make them ahead to have on hand if you get inspired at the last minute to do a special New Orleans dinner. They can also be used to spark up everyday dishes like steak, chicken, fish, or eggs. The Creole sauce that appears in the recipe for baked redfish, for example, is also delicious as a filling for omelets.

Timing is critical, so be sure to read the basic recipes carefully the day before to allow enough time to make the necessary stocks and sauces. Stocks, which cook from two to eight hours, can be made ahead and refrigerated or frozen.

If you are keeping a stock in the refrigerator, it is probably a good idea to boil it every three of four days to prevent bacteria from forming. You can also greatly intensify and enhance the flavor of your stocks—and your Creole dishes—by taking an already made stock and using it instead of water in the stock recipe, adding more bones, meat, vegetables, and seasoning. At Commander's, we cook our duck stock over a period of five days, continually adding more bones to achieve the very essence of an intense duck flavor.

One convenient way to keep stocks handy is to freeze them in ice-cube trays with individual plastic cups, then transfer the cubes to a tightly sealed container. This way you can take out as much or as little as you need at a time without having to defrost the whole quantity. Commander's special garlic butter can also be made in large quantities, frozen in a log, and sliced as you need it to add spirit to simple broiled or poached fish, steaks, and, of course, French bread.

Butter-based sauces, such as béarnaise or hollandaise can be made ahead, held warm in a preheated Thermos, and reheated just before serving.

Once you have mastered the basic Creole sauces, you will enjoy improvising and using them in new ways. Remember, experimentation and innovation are the heart and soul of Creole cookery.

Creole Seafood Seasoning

MAKES 2 CUPS

- 1/3 cup salt
- 1/4 cup granulated or powdered garlic
- 1/4 cup freshly ground black pepper
- 2 tablespoons cayenne pepper
- 2 tablespoons thyme
- 2 tablespoons oregano
- 1/3 cup paprika
- 3 tablespoons granulated or powdered onion

1 ■ Combine all ingredients and mix thoroughly.

2 ■ Pour into a large glass jar and seal airtight. Keeps indefinitely.

■ ***Note:*** If black pepper is not to your taste, reduce the quantity to half.

Creole Meat Seasoning

MAKES 3 CUPS

- 1 cup salt
- 3/4 cup granulated or powdered garlic
- 3/4 cup freshly ground black pepper
- 1/2 teaspoon cayenne pepper, or to taste
- 1/4 cup paprika

1 ■ Combine all ingredients and mix thoroughly.

2 ■ Pour into a large glass jar. Seal tightly. Keeps indefinitely.

Seafood Stock (including Shrimp, Crawfish, and Fish Stocks)

To each quart of water add:

- 1 medium onion, peeled and quartered
- 3 stalks celery, coarsely cut
- 1 whole clove garlic, peeled

1 This mixture should just cover a variety of good seafood stock makers, such as fresh shrimp heads and/or shells, or lobster heads and/or shells, any fresh fish bones, oyster liquor, or any combination of these. If shrimp, crawfish, or fish stock is called for, use the shells, bones, etc. of the particular fish specified.

2 Bring the ingredients to a rapid boil, then reduce heat to a slow simmer. Cook at least 2 hours, no more than 8. When making a stock, the best flavors are achieved by making the stock as clear as possible.

3 After stock is cooked, strain it, then reduce it for additional flavor. (If you have a sauce that calls for a small amount of liquid or stock but needs a lot of taste, reduction is necessary.) Take stock and pour it into a skillet or pot. Simmer, uncovered, until evaporation reduces it to half its original quantity. For instance, 1 quart good stock can be reduced to 1 cup or less by slow evaporation. In some instances 1 or 2 tablespoons of reduced stock make the difference between a mediocre and a fantastic dish.

Chicken/Duck Stock

MAKES 6 CUPS

- Carcasses of 4 chickens or ducks
- 2 medium carrots, sliced
- 2 medium onions, sliced
- 3 stalks celery, sliced
- 6 black peppercorns
- 3 quarts cold water

1 ■ For a brown chicken stock, preheat oven to 375°.

2 ■ Roast the bones, carrots, onions, and celery until very brown, about 45 minutes.

3 ■ Add bones, vegetables, and peppercorns to the water in a large soup kettle and bring to a rapid boil. Reduce heat to a gentle simmer and simmer for 4 hours.

4 ■ Strain stock, return to the kettle, and simmer until reduced to 6 cups.

■ ***Note:*** For a blond or white stock, do not brown bones and vegetables first.

Beef/Veal Stock

MAKES 2 QUARTS

- 2 beef or veal marrow bones, 4 inches in length
- Full rib bones, cracked
- 4 quarts cold water
- 2 medium onions, halved, with 2 cloves stuck in each half
- 3 stalks celery, coarsely cut
- 3 medium carrots, split
- 4 bay leaves
- ½ bunch fresh parsley
- 4 ounces stew meat

1 ■ Preheat oven to 400°.

2 ■ Scatter bones in bottom of a roasting pan and roast in the hot oven until brown, about 1 hour.

3 ■ Pour 2 quarts cold water into a 1-gallon stockpot and add the browned bones. Add onions, celery, carrots, bay leaves, parsley, and stew meat and bring to a rapid boil. Immediately turn heat down and simmer slowly over low heat for at least 2 to 4 hours. As the water evaporates, add more to keep the level at about 2 quarts.

4 ■ When cooked, remove from heat, strain, and cool. When cold, skim fat from surface.

Demi-glace

MAKES 3 CUPS

4 quarts Beef Stock (page 192)

1 Pour stock into large soup pot or kettle, bring to a boil, and cook over medium heat for 2 hours, or until reduced to 3 cups. Sauce will be thick and syrupy.

2 Refrigerate (it will keep about 7 days) or freeze.

Brown Sauce

MAKES ABOUT 3 CUPS

- 6 tablespoons oil
- 6 tablespoons all-purpose flour
- 1 quart (4 cups) Beef Stock (page 192)
- 2 fresh beef marrow bones, 6 inches long, cut into 2-inch sections
- 1 cup diced onions
- 2 teaspoons Worcestershire sauce
- 2 tablespoons tomato purée
- 2 bay leaves
- ½ teaspoon oregano
- 2 cloves of garlic, minced
- ½ teaspoon freshly ground black pepper
- ¼ teaspoon cayenne pepper
- 4 tablespoons Burgundy

1 In a small skillet heat oil over medium heat until very hot. Add flour, all at once, stirring, and continue to cook, stirring constantly, until roux is a very dark brown. Remove from heat and set aside.

2 Bring stock to a boil in a 6-quart saucepan. Add remaining ingredients, except the roux and wine, return to a boil, and simmer for 1¼ hours. Strain liquid, discarding the bones.

3 Return stock to the heat, add the roux, and whisk until well blended. Simmer for 15 minutes longer, stirring occasionally. Remove from heat and stir in the wine. Sauce will keep about 7 days in the refrigerator. Reheat in a double boiler.

Fish Brown Sauce

MAKES 1 CUP

This is an excellent sauce for dressing up a plain fish dish.

- 2 cups Fish Stock (page 191)
- ¼ cup diced onions
- 1 teaspoon Worcestershire sauce
- 1 bay leaf
- 1 clove of garlic
- Freshly ground black pepper, cayenne pepper, and salt to taste
- 1½ tablespoons oil
- 1½ tablespoons flour
- 2 tablespoons Burgundy

1 ■ Bring stock to a boil in a heavy pot. Add onions, Worcestershire sauce, bay leaf, garlic, black pepper, cayenne pepper, and salt. Lower heat and simmer for 1 hour.

2 ■ Heat oil in a small saucepan over medium heat. Whisk in flour and cook, whisking, until roux is smooth and brown in color, about 5 minutes. Remove from heat and set aside.

3 ■ When stock is finished simmering, add the roux and blend in well. Simmer an additional 30 minutes, stirring occasionally. Remove from heat and stir in wine.

4 ■ If not using sauce immediately, refrigerate and reheat in a double boiler.

Creole Meunière Sauce

MAKES 1½ CUPS

- 1 cup Brown Sauce (page 193)
- 8 tablespoons (1 stick) unsalted butter, cut into quarters
- 1 tablespoon Worcestershire sauce
- Juice of ½ lemon
- 2 tablespoons minced fresh parsley

1 ■ Bring brown sauce to a quick simmer in a heavy 1-quart saucepan. Add butter and Worcestershire sauce and whisk until butter is completely absorbed. Add lemon juice and again whisk until smooth.

2 ■ Remove from heat and stir in parsley.

■ ***Note:*** This sauce can be held for no more than 45 minutes. It should be kept at approximately 80 degrees in a double boiler over water.

Garlic Butter

MAKES ABOUT 3 POUNDS

This butter is delicious on broiled or poached fish, steak, hamburgers, broiled potatoes, canapés, and, of course, French bread.

- 8 cloves of garlic
- 2 pounds (8 sticks) unsalted butter
- 1/8 cup dry white wine
- 1/8 teaspoon oregano
- 2 tablespoons minced dill pickle
- 2 tablespoons minced parsley
- 4 tablespoons Pernod
- 1/8 teaspoon thyme
- 1/8 teaspoon sweet basil
- 2 anchovy fillets
- 1/2 small onion
- 1 teaspoon freshly ground black pepper
- Juice of 1 or 2 lemons

1 ■ For smoothest and best results, pound garlic to a paste with a pestle and gradually work butter into it. We find that a garlic press brings out an unappealing metallic flavor in the garlic.

2 ■ Put the pounded garlic and butter in a food processor. Add remaining ingredients and blend thoroughly with dough blade.

3 ■ Pack into a pottery crock or bowl and refrigerate, or freeze in a log to slice and use as needed.

Clarified or Drawn Butter

MAKES ABOUT 1 CUP

- 1/2 pound (2 sticks) unsalted butter

1 ■ Heat butter slowly in a heavy-bottomed saucepan until melted. Do not let it get too hot.

2 ■ Skim foam off surface and carefully pour the clear liquid off the sediment that has collected at bottom of saucepan. This clear liquid is the clarified butter. It will keep in the refrigerator for at least a week.

Béarnaise Sauce

MAKES 2½ CUPS

- ½ pound (2 sticks) unsalted butter
- 4 egg yolks, at room temperature
- Juice of 1 medium lemon
- 1½ teaspoons Worcestershire sauce
- Pinch of cayenne pepper
- 3 tablespoons Chablis or dry vermouth
- Salt to taste
- 2 teaspoons finely crumbled dried tarragon leaves

1 ■ Melt butter in a skillet over medium heat. Do not let it burn. When completely melted, remove from heat.

2 ■ Put egg yolks, lemon juice, Worcestershire sauce, and cayenne pepper in top of double boiler over simmering water. The water in the bottom pan should not touch the top pan.

3 ■ With a wire whisk, beat egg yolk mixture until it thickens and a sheen forms, approximately 3 minutes, but no more than 5. Begin adding melted butter in a steady stream, whisking constantly until all has been added. Add 2 tablespoons of the Chablis and whisk well. The sauce should be light and fluffy.

4 ■ In a small saucepan heat the remaining Chablis and the tarragon until liquid evaporates. Remove from heat and add the tarragon to the sauce, mixing well. Hold at room temperature until serving time.

Creole Sauce

MAKES 2 CUPS

- 2 tablespoons (¼ stick) unsalted butter
- 1 cup fine julienne strips onions
- 1 cup fine julienne strips green bell pepper
- 2 stalks celery, cut into fine julienne strips
- 2 cloves of garlic, thinly sliced
- 1 bay leaf
- 2 teaspoons paprika
- 2 cups diced tomatoes, fresh or canned
- 1 cup tomato juice
- 4 teaspoons Worcestershire sauce
- 4 teaspoons Louisiana Red Hot Sauce
- 1½ tablespoons cornstarch
- ½ cup water

1 Melt butter in a large skillet and sauté the vegetables with the garlic and bay leaf. Just before the onions become transparent add paprika, tomatoes, and tomato juice. Stir well.

2 Add Worcestershire sauce and hot sauce and simmer until sauce is reduced by a fourth, about 5 minutes.

3 Combine cornstarch and water and stir into sauce. Simmer until the cornstarch is cooked and sauce is glazed, about 2 minutes.

4 The sauce will keep four or five days in the refrigerator. In fact, it is better to make it a day ahead to allow the flavors to meld.

Choron Sauce

- 1 part Creole Sauce (page 197)
- 1 part Béarnaise Sauce (page 196)

In a heavy saucepan, reduce Creole sauce to half its original quantity. Add béarnaise sauce and mix well.

Béchamel Sauce (Medium-Thick Cream Sauce)

MAKES 1 CUP

- 2 tablespoons (¼ stick) unsalted butter
- 2 tablespoons all-purpose flour
- ¾ cup milk
- ¼ teaspoon freshly ground nutmeg
- ¼ teaspoon salt
- ½ teaspoon Louisiana Red Hot Sauce

1 ■ Melt butter in a heavy saucepan. Stir in flour and blend thoroughly.

2 ■ Gradually whisk in milk and continue to whisk over moderate heat until sauce is smooth and thickened.

3 ■ Add nutmeg, salt, and hot sauce. Whisk again and remove from heat.

4 ■ Sauce will keep about 7 days in the refrigerator. Reheat in a double boiler.

Marchand de Vins Sauce

MAKES 6 CUPS

- 4 tablespoons (½ stick) unsalted butter
- 1 cup finely diced ham
- 1 cup finely diced fresh mushrooms
- 1 cup finely chopped green onions
- 3 cups Demi-glace (page 193)
- 1½ cups red wine

1 ■ Melt butter in a heavy saucepan and sauté ham, mushrooms, and green onions until onions are transparent.

2 ■ Add demi-glace and wine, bring to a boil, and reduce by one quarter.

Hollandaise Sauce

MAKES 2½ CUPS

- ½ pound (2 sticks) unsalted butter
- 4 egg yolks, at room temperature
- Juice of 1 medium lemon
- 1½ teaspoons Worcestershire sauce
- Pinch of cayenne pepper
- 2 tablespoons Chablis or dry vermouth
- Salt to taste

1 Melt butter in a skillet over medium heat. Do not let burn. When completely melted, remove from heat.

2 Put egg yolks, lemon juice, Worcestershire sauce, and cayenne pepper in top of a double boiler over simmering water. The bottom of the upper pan should not touch the simmering water in the lower pan. Whisk yolks until mixture thickens and forms a sheen, approximately 3 minutes, no more than 5 minutes.

3 In a slow steady stream, add butter, whisking constantly until all butter has been added. Add the wine and whisk well. Sauce should be light and fluffy.

4 Hold sauce at room temperature until serving time.

Index

A

Absinthe
Frappé, 6
Suissesse, 4
Amaretto Freeze, 177
Anchovy Butter, Sliced Roast Tenderloin of Beef with, 148
Angel-Hair Pasta, Escargots with, 32
Appetizer(s), 15
Buster Crabs, 31
Crab Meat à la Marinière, 30–31
Crab Meat Ravigote, 30
Crawfish Mousse, 29
Crêpes Fruits de Mer, 22
Escargots with Angel-Hair Pasta, 32
Oysters à la Marinière, 23
Oyster and Crab Meat Ambrosia, 25
Oysters Commander, 26–27
Oyster Soufflé, 24–25
Oysters Palace, 28
Oysters Trufant, 27
Royale of Leeks and Mushrooms, 33
Shrimp and Mushroom Sauté, 19
Shrimp Croustade, 91
Shrimp Mousse, 20
Shrimp Remoulade, Commander's, 17
Shrimp Soufflé with Shrimp Sauce, 18–19
Tomato and Shrimp Aspic, 21
Artichoke(s)
in Eggs Sardou, 81
-Mushroom Sauce, 104
and Oysters Casserole, 112
in Oysters Commander, 26–27
Redfish with Mushrooms and, 104
Soup, Cream of, 43
Asparagus Soup, Cold, 44–45
Aspic, Tomato and Shrimp, 21
Avocado
and Crab Meat Salad, 53
Cream Parfait, 174
Soup, Cold, 45

B

Baked Alaska, Flaming, 175
Bananas Foster, 164
Béarnaise Sauce, 196
Béchamel Sauce, 198
Beef, 140–50
Filet Mignon Adelaide, 146
Filet Mignon Debris, 147
Filet Mignon Stanley, 145
Sliced Roast Tenderloin of, with Anchovy Butter, 148
Steak Diane with New Potatoes and Parsley Butter, 149
Stock, 192
Tenderloin with Tchoupitoulas Sauce, 150
Tournedos Coliseum, 145
Tournedos Provençale, 144
Beurre
Blanc, Creole, Charcoaled Flounder with, 118–19
Fondu, 108, 109
See also Butter
Bisque
Crab Meat and Corn, 36
Crawfish, 34–35
Bloody Mary, 11
Bouillabaisse, New Orleans, 116–17
Brandied Crisp Roast Duck with Peaches, 132–33
Brandy
Alexander, 10
Flip, 4
Bread
Garlic, Commander's, 16
Pudding, French, with Clear Rum Sauce, 168
Pudding Soufflé, with Whiskey Sauce, 168
Brennan Salad, 59
Brown Sauce, 193
Buster Crabs, 31
Butter
Anchovy, Sliced Roast Ten of Beef with, 148
Clarified or Drawn, 195
Garlic, 195
Lemon Sauce, 106
Parsley, Steak Diane with New Potatoes and, 149
Sauce, Lemon, 167
See also Beurre

C

Café, *see* Coffee
Calas (Rice Fritters), 74
California Salad, 65
Caramel Cup Custard, 180
Caramelized Sugar, 180
Catfish, Deep-Fried, 117
Celebration Dessert, 176
Chablis Cassis, 10

Champagne Ice, 172
Chapon Dressing, 58
Charcoaled Flounder with Beurre Blanc, 118–19
Chicken, 120–27
Crêpes Clair, 127
in Gumbo Ya Ya, 38
in Jambalaya, 115
Margaux, 126
Pontalba, 125
Salad, Fried, 67
Salad with Fresh Fruit, 66–67
in Senegalese Soup, 47
Stock, 192
Tarragon, Breasts of, 124
Chocolate
-Coated Chocolate Truffles, 184
Mousse, 178
Mousse, White, 178–79
Choron Sauce, 99, 197
Clarified Butter, 195
Coconut Beer Shrimp with Sweet and Tangy Dipping Sauce, 90
Coffee
Café au Lait, 186
Café au Lait Soufflé, 170
Café Brûlot, 186
Café Noir, 186
Café Pierre, 187
Irish, 187
Commander's Dressing, 52
Commander's Endive and Walnut Salad, 60
Commander's French Dressing, 53
Commander's Garlic Bread, 16
Commander's Homemade Sausage, 72
Commander's Louis Dressing, 55
Commander's Marinated Vegetable Salad, 58
Commander's Salad, 52
Commander's Shrimp Remoulade, 17
Corn Bisque, Crab Meat and, 36
Coulibiac of Redfish, Creole, 108–9
Crab(s) (Crab Meat)
à la Marinière, 30–31
and Avocado Salad, 53
Buster, 31
Cakes, Deviled, 78–79
and Corn Bisque, 36
Imperial, 98
Lausaune, 97
Louis, Fresh Lump, 55
in Neptune Salad, 54
Omelet, 83
and Oyster Ambrosia, 25
in Oysters Palace, 28
Ravigote, 30
Sautéed, Redfish Grieg with, 103
in Seafood Gumbo, 37
Soft-Shell, Choron, 99
Stock, 36
Crawfish
Bisque, 34–35
to boil, 34, 35
Mousse, 29
and Pasta with Stir-Fried Vegetables, 93
to purge, 34
Rice, 94
Sauté of Fresh Louisiana, 94
Stock, 34, 35, 191
Cream Sauce, Ham, 72
Cream of Artichoke Soup, 43
Cream of Eggplant Soup, 46
Creamy Green Onion Dressing, 57
Creole Beurre Blanc, Charcoaled Flounder with, 118–19
Creole Coulibiac of Redfish, 108–9
Creole Cream Cheese Ice Cream, 177
Creole Meat Seasoning, 190
Creole Meunière Sauce, 194
Oysters en Brochette with, 114
Redfish in, 105
Trout with Roasted Pecans and, 96–97
Creole Mustard Sauce with Herbs, 117
Creole Onion Soup, 42
Creole Sauce, 77, 197
Creole Seafood Seasoning, 190
Creole Tomato Soup, 46
Crêpes, 164
Clair, 127
Fruits de Mer, 22
Kovacs, 166–67
Lemon, 167
Soufflé Praline, 171
Suzette, 164–65
Custard
Caramel Cup, 180
Royale of Leeks and Mushrooms, 33
Sauce, 166

D

Demi-glace, 193
Desserts, 160–85
Amaretto Freeze, 177
Avocado Cream Parfait, 174
Bananas Foster, 164
Bread Pudding Soufflé with Whiskey Sauce, 168
Café au Lait Soufflé, 170
Caramel Cup Custard, 180

Celebration Dessert, 176
Champagne Ice, 172
Chocolate Mousse, 178
Chocolate-Coated Chocolate Truffles, 184
Creole Cream Cheese Ice Cream, 177
Crêpes Kovacs, 166–67
Crêpes Soufflé Praline, 171
Crêpes Suzette, 164–65
Flaming Baked Alaska, 175
Floating Island, 181
French Bread Pudding with Clear Rum Sauce, 168
French Vanilla Ice Cream, 172
Lemon Crêpes, 167
Lemon Mousse, 179
Pecan Bourbon Balls, 185
Pecan Pie, 183
Poached Pears in Pistachio Sauce, 182
Praline Parfait, 173
Pralines, 185
Strawberries Romanoff, 174
White Chocolate Mousse, 178–79
Deviled Crab Cakes, 78–79
Dill Mayonnaise, 56
Dipping Sauce, Sweet and Tangy, Coconut Beer Shrimp with, 90
Dirty Rice, Roast Quail with, 134–35
Dressing, Salad, *see* Salad Dressing
Drinks (cocktails), 3–11
Absinthe Frappé, 6
Absinthe Suissesse, 4
Bloody Mary, 11
Brandy Alexander, 10
Brandy Flip, 4
daytime, 3, 3
Kir or Chablis Cassis, 10
Kir Royale, 11
Milk Punch, 9
Mint Julep, 8
Negroni, 9
Ojen Cocktail, 6
Ojen Frappé, 6
Planter's Punch, 5
Ramos Gin Fizz, 7
Rickey, 10
Sazerac Cocktail, 5
Sidecar Cocktail, 7
Singapore Sling, 8
Duck
Brandied Crisp Roast, with Peaches, 132–33
and Fettuccine, 131
Jambalaya, 129
Pressed, 122, 128
Roast, with Green Peppercorns, 130
Salad, 64–65
Stock, 192
Stock, Rich, 132, 133
Duxelles, Mushroom, 108

E

Eggplant
in Eggs Elizabeth, 80
Soup, Cream of, 46
Eggs, 68–83
Basin Street, 74
Benedict, 73
Commander, 72–73
Cordon Bleu, 79
Crab Meat Omelet, 83
Creamed Oyster Omelet, 82
Creole, 77
de la Salle, 78–79
Elizabeth, 80
Four Egg Omelet, 82
Hussard, 75
St. Charles, 75
Sardou, 81
Soubise, 76
Endive and Walnut Salad, Commander's, 6
Escargot(s)
with Angel-Hair Pasta, 32
Soup, 39

F

Fettuccine
Duck and, 131
Panéed Veal and, 151
Shrimp and, 88
Filet Mignon
Adelaide, 146
Debris, 147
Stanley, 145
Fish
Brown Sauce, 194
Stock, 191
See also specific types of fish
Floating Island, 181
Flounder
Charcoaled, with Beurre Blanc, 118–19
Stuffed, 119
Forcemeat Stuffing, 146
Frappé
Absinthe, 6
Ojen, 6
French Bread Pudding with Clear Rum Sauce, 168

French Dressing, Commander's, 53
French Vanilla Ice Cream, 172
Fruit, Chicken Salad with, 66–67

G

Game birds, 122
  See also Duck; Goose; Pigeon; Quail
Garlic
  Bread, Commander's, 16
  Butter, 195
  oil, 58
  Vinaigrette Dressing, 61
Gin Fizz, Ramos, 7
Goose
  Cranberry Relish for, 139
  Roast, with Red Cabbage and Apple, 136–37
Gravy, Giblet Mushroom, Roast Turkey with Oyster Dressing and, 138–39
Green Onion Dressing, Creamy, 57
Grits, Fried, 77
Gumbo, xv
  Seafood, 37
  Ya Ya, 38

H

Ham
  Cream Sauce, 72
  in Eggs Cordon Bleu, 79
Herb(s)
  Dressing, 59
  Mustard Sauce with, Creole, 117
Hollandaise Sauce, 199
Honey-Yogurt Dressing, 65

I

Ice, Champagne, 172
Ice Cream
  Creole Cream Cheese, 177
  French Vanilla, 172
Irish Coffee, 187

J

Jambalaya, 115
  Duck, 129

K

Kir, 10
  Royale, 11

L

Lafayette Sauce, 157
Leek(s)
  Royale of Mushrooms and, 33
  Sauce, Trout in, 95
Lemon
  Butter Sauce, 167
  Crêpes, 167
  Mousse, 179
Louis Dressing, Commander's, 55

M

Marchand de Vins Sauce, 198
Mayonnaise
  Dill, 56
  Homemade, 66
  Tarragon-Shallot, 54
Meunière Sauce, Creole, 194
  Oysters en Brochette with, 114
  Redfish in, 105
  Trout with Roasted Pecans and, 96–97
Milk Punch, 9
Mint Julep, 8
Mousse
  Crawfish, 29
  Lemon, 179
  Seafood, Whole Redfish Stuffed with, 110
  Shrimp, 20
  White Chocolate, 178–79
Mushroom(s)
  -Artichoke Sauce, 104
  Duxelles, 108, 109
  -Giblet Sauce, Roast Turkey with Oyster Dressing and, 138–39
  Morel Soup, 42
  Redfish with Artichokes and, 104
  Royale of Leeks and, 33
  Sauce, Wild, 78–79
  and Shrimp Sauté, 19
  Wild, Veal with, 158
Mustard Sauce with Herbs, Creole, 117

N

Negroni, 9
Neptune Salad, 54

O

Ojen
  Frappé, 6
  Cocktail, 6
Onion Soup, Creole, 42
Oyster(s)
  à la Marinière, 23
  and Artichoke Casserole, 112
  Commander, 26–27
  Commander Sauce, 26
  and Crab Meat Ambrosia, 25
  Dressing, Roast Turkey with Giblet Mushroom Sauce and, 138–39
  Dressing, Veal Roast Stuffed with, 156–57
  en Brochette, 114
  Omelet, Creamed, 82
  Palace, 28
  Patties, 113
  Sauce, for Oyster Soufflé, 24
  in Seafood Gumbo, 37
  Soufflé, 24–25
  Soup with Pastry Dome, 41
  Trufant, 27

P

Panéed Veal and Fettuccine, 151
Papillote Sauce, 100
Parfait
  Avocado Cream, 174
  Praline, 173
Pasta
  Angel-Hair, Escargots with, 32
  Crawfish and, 93
  Duck and Fettuccine, 131
  Panéed Veal and Fettuccine, 151
  Salad, 61
  Shrimp and Fettuccine, 88
Pâté de Foie Gras, Tenderloin of Veal Citron with, 159
Peaches, Brandied Crisp Roast Duck with, 132–33
Pears, Poached, in Pistachio Sauce, 18
Pecan(s)
  Bourbon Balls, 185
  Pie, 183
  Trout with Roasted Pecans and Creole Meunière Sauce, 96–97
Pesto, as garnish for soups, 44
Pie
  Crust, Basic, 183
  Pecan, 183
Pigeon, Grilled Louisiana, 137
Pistachio Sauce, Poached Pears in, 182
Planter's Punch, 5
Poached Pears in Pistachio Sauce, 182
Pompano
  en Papillotte, 87, 100–101
  Grand Duc, 101
Potato(es)
  New, Steak Diane with Parsley Butter and, 149
  Soup, Cold (Vichyssoise), 44
Praline(s), 185
  Crêpes Soufflé, 171
  Parfait, 173
Pressed Duck, 122, 128
Puff pastry
  Oyster Soup with Dome of, 41
  Shrimp Croustade in, 91

Q

Quail, Roast, with Dirty Rice, 134–35

R

Ramos Gin Fizz, 7
Raspberry Sauce, 178
Ravigote Sauce, 63
Red Beans and Rice, in Eggs Basin Street, 74
Red Cabbage and Apples, with Roast Goose, 136–37
Redfish
  with Artichokes and Mushrooms, 104
  Court-Bouillon, Baked, 105
  Creole Coulibiac of, 108–9
  in Crole Meunière Sauce, 105
  Grieg, 103
  Grilled, 86–87, 106–7
  Orleans, 111
  au Poivre, 107
  with Shrimp, 102
  Stuffed with Seafood Mousse, Whole, 110
Remoulade
  Sauce, 62
  Shrimp, Commander's, 17
Rice
  Crawfish, 94
  Dirty, Roast Quail with, 134–35
  Fritters (Calas), 74
  Pilaf, 108, 109
Rickey, 10
Rum Sauce, Clear, 168

S

Salad(e), 48–57
  Brennan, 59
  California, 65
  Chatelaine, 56
  Chicken, Fried, 67
  Chicken, with Fresh Fruit, 66–67
  Commander's, 52
  Commander's Marinated Vegetable, 58
  Crab Meat and Avocado, 53
  Duck, 64–65
  Fontaine, 56
  Fresh Lump Crab Meat, 55
  Gourmande, 57
  Neptune, 54
  Pasta, 61
  Shrimp, I, 62
  Shrimp, II, 63
Salad Dressing
  Chapon, 58
  Commander's, 52
  Commander's French, 53
  Commander's Louis, 55
  Creamy Green Onion, 57
  Garlic Vinaigrette, 61
  Herb, 59
  Honey-Yogurt, 65
  Special Fried Chicken Salad, 67
  Walnut, 60
Sauce(s)
  Artichoke Mushroom, 104
  Béarnaise, 196
  Béchamel, 198
  Brown, 193
  Cheese, 151
  Choron, 99, 197
  Clear Rum, 168
  Creole, 77, 197
  Creole Meunière, 194
  Creole Meunière, Oysters en Brochette with, 114
  Creole Meunière, Redfish in, 105
  Creole Meunière, Trout with Roasted Pecans and, 96–97
  Creole Mustard, with Herbs, 117
  Custard, 166
  Fish Brown, 194
  Ham Cream, 72
  Hollandaise, 199
  Lafayette, 157
  Leek, Trout in, 95
  Lemon Butter, 106, 167
  Marchand de Vins, 198
  Oyster, for Oyster Soufflé, 24
  Oysters Commander, 26
  Papillotte, 100
  Pistachio, Poached Pears in, 182
  Quail, 134, 135
  Raspberry, 178
  Ravigote, 63
  Remoulade, 62
  Shrimp, Shrimp Soufflé with, 18–19
  Soubise, 76
  Sweet and Tangy Dipping, Coconut Beer Shrimp with, 90
  Tchoupitoulas, Beef Tenderloin with, 150
  Whiskey, Bread Pudding Soufflé with, 168
  Wild Mushroom, 78–79
Sausage
  andouille, in Gumbo Ya Ya, 38
  Commander's Homemade, 72
  in Eggs Creole, 77
  in Eggs Soubise, 76
Sauté of Fresh Louisiana Crawfish, 94
Sazerac Cocktail, 5
Scallops, in Neptune Salad, 54
Seafood, 84–119
  Crêpes Fruits de Mer, 22
  Gumbo, 37
  Mousse, Whole Redfish Stuffed with, 110
  in Neptune Salad, 54
  Seasoning, Creole, 190
  Stock, 191
  See also specific types of seafood
Seasoning(s)
  Creole Meat, 190
  Creole Seafood, 190
Senegalese Soup, 47
Shallot-Tarragon Mayonnaise, 54
Shellfish, *see specific types of shellfish*
Shrimp
  Coconut Beer, with Sweet and Tangy Dippping Sauce, 90
  Creole, 92
  Croustade, 91
  and Fettuccine, 88
  in Jambalaya, 115
  Mousse, 20
  and Mushroom Sauté, 19
  in Neptune Salad, 54
  Redfish with, 102
  Remoulade, Commander's, 17
  Salad I, 62
  Salad II, 63
  Sauce, Shrimp Soufflé with, 18–19
  in Seafood Gumbo, 37
  Soufflé, with Shrimp Sauce, 18–19
  Stock, 191
  and Tomato Aspic, 21
  Victoria, 89

Sidecar Cocktail, 7
Singapore Sling, 8
Snails, *see* Escargot(s)
Soft-Shell Crab Choron, 99
Soubise Sauce, 76
Soufflé, xv
  Bread Pudding, with Whiskey Sauce, 168
  Café au Lait, 170
  Oyster, 24–25
  Praline, Crêpes, 171
  Shrimp, with Shrimp Sauce, 18–19
Soup, 39–47
  about, 15
  Cold Asparagus, 44–45
  Cold Avocado, 45
  Cold Potato (Vichyssoise), 44
  Cold Watercress, 45
  Cream of Artichoke, 43
  Cream of Eggplant, 46
  Escargot, 39
  Morel, 42
  Onion, Creole, 42
  Oyster, with Pastry Dome, 41
  Senegalese, 47
  Tomato, Creole, 46
  Turtle, 40
  See also Bisque; Gumbo
Spinach, Creamed, 81
Steak Diane with New Potatoes and Parsley Butter, 149
Stock(s), xv
  Beef or Veal, 192
  Chicken or Duck, 192
  Crab, 36
  Crawfish, 34, 35
  Duck, Rich, 132, 133
  Seafood, 191
Strawberries Romanoff, 174
Stuffing
  Crawfish Head, 34–35
  Forcemeat, 146
  for Oysters Commander, 26
Sugar, Caramelized, 180
Syrup, simple, 4

T

Tarragon-Shallot Mayonnaise, 54
Tchoupitoulas Sauce, Beef Tenderloin with, 150
Tenderloin of Veal Citron with Pâté de Foie Gras, 159
Tomato(es)
  and Shrimp Aspic, 21
  Soup, Creole, 46
Trout
  in Eggs St. Charles, 75
  in Leek Sauce, 95
  with Roasted Pecans and Creole Meunière Sauce, 96–97
Truffles, Chocolate-Coated Chocolate, 184
Turkey
  Cranberry Relish for, 139
  Roast, with Oyster Dressing and Giblet Mushroom Sauce, 138–39
Turtle Soup, 40

V

Vanilla Ice Cream, French, 172
Veal
  Calvados, 154
  Citron with Pâté de Foie Gras, Tenderloin of, 159
  Grillades, 155
  Kottwitz, 152
  Lafayette, 157
  Marcelle, 153
  Panéed, and Fettuccine, 151
  Roast Stuffed, with Oyster Dressing, 156–57
  with Wild Mushrooms, 158
Vegetables, *see* Salads; *and specific vegetables*
Vichyssoise (Cold Potato Soup), 44
Vinaigrette Dressing, Garlic, 61

W

Walnut
  and Endive Salad, Commander's, 60
  Dressing, 60
Watercress
  Salade Chatelaine, 56
  Soup, Cold, 45
Whiskey Sauce, Bread Pudding Soufflé with, 168
White Chocolate Mousse, 178–79
Wild Mushroom Sauce, 78–79

Y

Yams Richard, 139
Yogurt, Honey Dressing, 65